Lecture Notes in Computer Science 13470

More information about this series at https://link.springer.com/bookseries/8637

Abdelkader Hameurlain ·
A Min Tjoa (Eds.)

Transactions on Large-Scale Data- and Knowledge- Centered Systems LII

Springer

Editors-in-Chief
Abdelkader Hameurlain
IRIT, Paul Sabatier University
Toulouse, France

A Min Tjoa
IFS, Technical University of Vienna
Vienna, Austria

ISSN 0302-9743   ISSN 1611-3349 (electronic)
Lecture Notes in Computer Science
ISSN 1869-1994   ISSN 2510-4942 (electronic)
Transactions on Large-Scale Data- and Knowledge-Centered Systems
ISBN 978-3-662-66145-1   ISBN 978-3-662-66146-8 (eBook)
https://doi.org/10.1007/978-3-662-66146-8

This Springer imprint is published by the registered company Springer-Verlag GmbH, DE,
part of Springer Nature
The registered company address is: Heidelberger Platz 3, 14197 Berlin, Germany

Preface

This volume contains six fully revised regular papers, covering a wide range of very hot topics in the fields of decryption keys management, delegations as a rights management system, data analytics in connected environments, knowledge graph augmentation, online optimized product quantization for All-Nearest-Neighbors Queries, generalization of argument models, and transactional modeling using coverage pattern mining, selected for this TLDKS volume. The last three papers of this volume, selected by the Program Committee Co-chairs of DEXA 2021, are extended versions where the short versions were published in the proceedings of the 32nd International Conference on Database and Expert Systems Applications (DEXA 2021).

We would like to sincerely thank the editorial board and the external reviewers for thoroughly refereeing the submitted papers and ensuring the high quality of this volume. Furthermore, we would like to wholeheartedly thank the Springer team for their ready availability, management efficiency, and very pleasant collaboration in the realization of the TLDKS journal volumes.

July 2022

Abdelkader Hameurlain
A Min Tjoa

Organization

Editors-in-Chief

Abdelkader Hameurlain   Paul Sabatier University, IRIT, France
A Min Tjoa   TU Wien, Austria

Editorial Board

Reza Akbarinia	Inria, France
Dagmar Auer	Johannes Kepler University Linz, Austria
Djamal Benslimane	University of Lyon 1, France
Stéphane Bressan	National University of Singapore, Singapore
Mirel Cosulschi	University of Craiova, Romania
Johann Eder	Alpen Adria University of Klagenfurt, Austria
Stefano Ferilli	University of Bari, Italy
Anna Formica	National Research Council, Italy
Shahram Ghandeharizadeh	University of Southern California, USA
Anastasios Gounaris	Aristotle University of Thessaloniki, Greece
Sergio Ilarri	University of Zaragoza, Spain
Petar Jovanovic	Universitat Politècnica de Catalunya and BarcelonaTech, Spain
Aida Kamišalić Latifić	University of Maribor, Slovenia
Dieter Kranzlmüller	Ludwig-Maximilians-Universität München, Germany
Philippe Lamarre	INSA Lyon, France
Lenka Lhotská	Czech Technical University in Prague, Czech Republic
Vladimir Marik	Czech Technical University in Prague, Czech Republic
Jorge Martinez Gil	Software Competence Center Hagenberg, Austria
Franck Morvan	Paul Sabatier University, IRIT, France
Torben Bach Pedersen	Aalborg University, Denmark
Günther Pernul	University of Regensburg, Germany
Viera Rozinajova	Kempelen Institute of Intelligent Technologies, Slovakia
Soror Sahri	LIPADE, Université Paris Cité, France
Joseph Vella	University of Malta, Malta
Shaoyi Yin	Paul Sabatier University, IRIT, France
Feng "George" Yu	Youngstown State University, USA

External Reviewers

Sven Groppe	University of Lübeck, Germany
Ionut Emil Iacob	Georgia Southern University, USA
Michal Kratky	Technical University of Ostrava, Czech Republic

Petr Křemen   Czech Technical University in Prague, Czech Republic
Elio Masciari   University Federico II of Naples, Italy
Riad Mokadem   Paul Sabatier University, IRIT, France
Gheorghe Cosmin Silaghi   Babes-Bolyai University, Romania

Contents

Mutida: A Rights Management Protocol for Distributed Storage Systems Without Fully Trusted Nodes

Bastien Confais[1]([✉]), Gustavo Rostirolla[1], Benoît Parrein[2], Jérôme Lacan[3], and François Marques[1]

[1] Inatysco, 30 ruc de l'Aiguillerie, 34000 Montpellier, France
{bastien.confais,gustavo.rostirolla,francois.marques}@inatysco.fr
[2] Nantes Université, Polytech Nantes, rue Christian Pauc, BP50609, 44306 Nantes, France
benoit.parrein@univ-nantes.fr
[3] ISAE Supaero, 10, Avenue Édouard-Belin, BP 54032, 31055 Toulouse, France
jerome.lacan@isae-supaero.fr

Abstract. Several distributed storage solutions that do not rely on a central server have been proposed over the last few years. Most of them are deployed on public networks on the internet. However, these solutions often do not provide a mechanism for access rights to enable the users to control who can access a specific file or piece of data. In this article, we propose Mutida (from the Latin word "Aditum" meaning "access"), a protocol that allows the owner of a file to delegate access rights to another user. This access right can then be delegated to a computing node to process the piece of data. The mechanism relies on the encryption of the data, public key/value pair storage to register the access control list and on a function executed locally by the nodes to compute the decryption key. After presenting the mechanism, its advantages and limitations, we show that the proposed mechanism has similar functionalities to Wave, an authorization framework with transitive delegation. However, Wave does not require fully trusted nodes. We implement our approach in a Java software program and evaluate it on the Grid'5000 testbed. We compare our approach to an approach based on a protocol relying on Shamir key reconstruction, which provides similar features.

1 Introduction

Currently, there are several distributed storage solutions that either rely on a central metadata server used to locate the data replicas or use a peer-to-peer (P2P) protocol that is suitable for deployment on public networks with nodes that are not necessarily trusted. When a trusted metadata server is present, it is relatively easy to manage the access rights [41]; the server checks if the user is allowed to access the file before distributing the location. In a full P2P

© Springer-Verlag GmbH Germany, part of Springer Nature 2022
A. Hameurlain and A. M. Tjoa (Eds.): *Transactions on Large-Scale Data- and Knowledge-Centered Systems LII*, LNCS 13470, pp. 1–34, 2022.
https://doi.org/10.1007/978-3-662-66146-8_1

network [25, 38], with untrusted nodes and pieces of data that are publicly accessible, managing access rights poses a different challenge. The main challenge is that there are no servers that we can rely on to be in charge of the protocol for rights management. Additionally, anonymity is a key point since peers are communicating directly and additional layers need to be in place to guarantee it [19]. In this paper, we propose Mutida (from the Latin word "Aditum" meaning "access" and written from right to left), a protocol that focuses on enabling users to manage access rights in a network of the second category.

In this paper, we consider the files stored on the Interplanetary File System [11] (IPFS), which is a storage solution that relies on a BitTorrent-like [35] protocol to exchange the files between the nodes and on a Kademlia [39] Distributed Hash Table (DHT) to locate the different pieces of data in the network. The essential characteristic of IPFS is that files are immutable and cannot be modified once they are written.

Using a DHT forwards all location requests through different nodes. Therefore, any connected node is involved in the routing of requests and can determine the identifiers of popular files [26]. Additionally, since the storage solution does not manage any permission and because IPFS does not provide any encryption mechanism to protect user privacy [47], every user can access all the files stored in it if the content identifier (CID) is known.

The consequence of this is that any node in the IPFS network can observe the DHT requests and access the corresponding files. This illustrates and justifies the need to manage access permissions in such a network. With Mutida, all users will still be able to find the files in the network, but only the permitted users will be able to decrypt the content.

Because of the use of Merkle trees [40] and the use of a root hash as a file identifier, users of IPFS do not need to trust the storage nodes to be assured that the retrieved file has not been tampered with. In our protocol, to manage access rights, we rely on the same level of trust; the exchanged messages are protected against any disclosure to a third party and are not corrupted on the path. However, the nodes themselves can be malicious and cannot necessarily behave as expected. They may go offline with no warning. One essential requirement of our proposition is that the owner of a file can delegate its access permission to another user. Similarly, computing nodes should be able to access and decrypt pieces of data when a user requests them to process their own data.

In Mutida, the files are encrypted before being stored in the distributed data storage solution. Then, a public Access Control List (ACL) and a local function that can be executed by each client are used to determine the key required to decrypt the file. The ACL consists of key/value storage deployed in the same network. The values are public, and the modifications can be controlled by trusted nodes or consensus algorithms. We also mention that a detailed security analysis of the proposed mechanism is beyond the scope of this paper. Additionally, data access revocation is contemplated in Mutida but not guaranteed. Ensuring revocation in a distributed manner is explored in [14, 32] or legally in [33]. The main contributions of this article are as follows:

- a method for data access control based on a function executed locally on the client;
- a delegation mechanism to distribute access rights to users or to the nodes that we want to allow permission to process the data;
- a performance comparison with a solution based on key splitting, including the impact of network limitations on each method.

It is the protocol to manage decryption keys and delegations, thought it does not directly provide functionalities of authentication, authorization verification or accountability. Our approach uses common cryptographic functions to build the desired features, and its novelty resides in the way that these functions are combined to form a new protocol for right management.

The remainder of this paper is organized as follows: In Sect. 2 we present the related work. In Sects. 3 and 4, we introduce the usage scenarios and the Mutida model, followed by Sects. 5 and 6, where we provide the methodology and the results obtained. Finally, in Sect. 7, we present the paper conclusions as well as directions for future works.

2 Related Work

The majority of the approaches that deal with the problem of managing access rights in a distributed environment rely on data encryption. This problem is relevant in a wide variety of domains, such as healthcare [31], data sharing [3] and administrative environments [17]. Several approaches, including a subset that is detailed below, can be found in the literature. However, to the best of our knowledge, none of the proposed methods allows an access right delegation mechanism in a P2P manner with a specificity to grant compute nodes a temporary permission to access data on behalf of the user requesting the computation. In our case, we follow the delegation definition of Gasser and McDermott [21], which describes the process where a user in a distributed environment authorizes a system to access remote resources on their behalf. We also highlight that in most of the works where the file key is exchanged through re-encryption using a public key, such as [29,30] and [51], the key is generally known by a given group, and thus, the file owner could give access even without the users consent or demand.

In 2008, Jawad et al. [29] proposed a solution where files are stored in encrypted form. The user must then communicate directly with the owner of the data to obtain the key. The clear limitation of this approach is that it requires the presence and simultaneous connection to the network of the owner of the piece of data and the user wishing to access it. This constraint is present in many other propositions, as emphasized by Yang et al. [61]. Moreover, sometimes the key exchange involves a trusted third party [3]. Adya et al. [1] remedied this constraint by proposing to create a data replica per user. Giving authorization to a user to access the data entails creating a new replica encrypted with the user's public key. As a result, the user and the owner do not have to meet to exchange keys, but the price to pay is a substantial increase in the use of storage space.

Another proposal is to manage the keys within a blockchain [10,52,54] instead of a trusted third party. For Steichen et al. [54], the blockchain was used to store the access control list. Storage nodes were responsible for consulting it before distributing data to the user. The major disadvantage of the approach was that it assumed that the storage nodes are trusted enough to not deliver data to unauthorized people. Similarly, Battah et al. [10] proposed the addition of a multiparty authorization (MPA) scheme, which was also stored in a smart contract to ensure that a single malicious party could not act alone. The consequence of this scheme was that the whole approach relied on proxy re-encryption nodes associated with a reputation scheme, as well as shared keys among the parties where a minimum number must be collected to access the file decryption key, thus increasing the complexity and time for the exchanges to take place.

To overcome this, Sari and Sipos [51] proposed an approach where data is encrypted with a symmetric key. This symmetric key is encrypted with the user's public key and stored in the blockchain. Xu et al. [60] corrected the trust problem by not only using the blockchain to store the access control list but also by implementing the verification of access rights within smart contracts. The idea is that the nodes of the blockchain come to a consensus on whether a user can access the requested data and issue them the key. The disadvantages of such an approach include the induced latency due to the use of a distributed consensus and the blockchain being an append-only data structure. Thus, it can be a space problem when access changes regularly: new users are allowed, and others have their permission revoked. Attribute encryption [58] and proxy re-encryption [15] are also two other approaches that have been proposed. The first required complex key management and the second required trust in the machine that adapted the encrypted data to the user's key.

Alternatively, broadcast encryption [30] is an encryption technique that consists of encrypting content for a group of users. Each user has a unique set of keys. A set of keys is used in encryption that allows only a specific group of users to decrypt the data. This system works well when there are few different groups and each group has numerous users. In this case, the number of managed keys is lower than the classic solution using ACLs. In addition, each piece of data is accessible by a unique group of users, which would lead to the use of a large number of keys. The main flaw shared by most of these solutions is that they do not allow permission delegation. A user who has obtained the rights to the owner's data cannot authorize a machine to access this data as part of the execution of a computation. The other limitation is anonymity; access control lists make it clear who can access what data.

Beyond encryption to manage access rights, some protocols are dedicated to key management and delegation. Lesueur et al. [36] proposed building a Public Key Infrastructure (PKI) in a P2P manner. Their protocol relies on key splitting and partial signatures. This was a major advance in the sense that it enabled distributed decisions to be made. For instance, nodes can agree to sign the public key of a new user so that it can be trusted or to sign any request that requires a consensus, such as a request to access a certain piece of data. The major drawback of this proposal is that it is difficult to manage redundancy in key parts and to react when a certain number of nodes leave the network simultaneously. This idea of distributed signatures was used by Wang et al. [59] to manage the access rights of data.

Some articles proposed protocols considering specific problems of the right management in a distributed solution. For instance, Tran, Hitchens and Varadharajan [28] considered trusting the nodes because some nodes can act in a malicious way. Similar to our context with data immutability, we have the content protection of recordable media (CPRM) [23], where the data cannot be modified. However, the main difference between the protocols is that in our approach, the access rights should not be given without the request of a user.

Wave [4] is one of the rare protocols that focuses on permission delegation in distributed applications. The protocol has the specificity that it does not require any centralization by relying on a blockchain-like solution to store the access rights. Nevertheless, Wave is more focused on rights management for applications. In their case, the nodes that provide the service must check if the client has the right to access a given service. While that is feasible in the service context, it would be a blocking point for storage components such as IPFS, meaning that it would need to be modified to verify the rights before delivering the content. For us, the nodes do not deliver a service besides data, and therefore, we cannot trust these nodes to manage the rights.

As in our protocol, Wave allows users to create delegation chains with an anonymity on the created delegations. When a user requests a permission to a node, the node granting the permission sends a record to the user and stores a second record encrypted in the blockchain. The external users cannot determine the permissions by reading the blockchain content, but a specific node to which the users send the record is able to verify the validity of the chain delegation from the blockchain. The difference from our protocol and its main drawback is that the permission check is performed by the node delivering the service. This difference implies that Wave requires that the nodes delivering the services be trusted nodes. Some proposals, such as Aura et al. [7], used a more straightforward implementation using the signature of certificates, similar to what it is used in Public Key Infrastructure.

Access revocation is also an entire topic to discuss. Revocation has always been a difficult problem in distributed solutions. One of the best examples of this is that certificate revocation in browsers trusting different authorities still does not have an ideal solution [16]. In distributed storage solutions, common solutions rely on a distributed consensus [34] and generally use a blockchain, but it is sometimes not enough for a single node to make the decision to deliver the piece of data to a user. In this case, Schnitzler et al. [52] proposed an incentive to the nodes to revoke the access and delete the pieces of data when needed, but it does not guarantee that Byzantine faults are avoided.

In other commercially available approaches for authentication and authorization, such as Kerberos [41] and Oauth [24], the user contacts a server that delivers a token used to access different services. The server delivering the token can be seen as an ACL server (similar to the one described in Sect. 4), and then the token is used to connect different storage nodes that can send the data. However, these models imply trust in the server delivering the service.

Finally, some papers focused on the problematic of anonymity. This means that the nodes should not be able to establish a list of the files a user can access. Backes et al. [8] proposed such a solution where nodes can only determine if the user sending a request is allowed to access the piece of data or not, without revealing any piece of information about the user.

We propose Mutida to fill the gap with a method that allows an access right delegation mechanism in a P2P manner with a specificity for delegations to compute nodes that have a temporary permission to access data on behalf of the user requesting the computation. Our method allows the management, delegation and revocation of rights over a file in a distributed P2P system. The goal is to allow the users to recreate all the file keys that they have access to with a single local function and a key pair. The usage scenarios and assumptions for Mutida, as well as a detailed model description, are presented in the following sections.

3   Usage Scenarios and Assumptions

The first use case we target is a user who stores their own data on their own IPFS node. Assuming that the user wants to be the only person to access their data, the right management protocol should protect the data against unauthorized access and should not have a strong overhead.

The second use case targeted is when the user wants to be able to share the data with another user. The other user sends a request to the owner to obtain permission to access the file. The owner accepts the request and enables this second user to compute the decryption key of the file.

The third use case is a situation where a user that is allowed to access a piece of data should be able to ask a computing node for processing the data. For this, the user should be able to temporarily give permission to the compute node to access and decrypt the file. These two last use cases indicate that the solution should have a delegation mechanism with the following properties:

i) The owner of a piece of data is the only user who decides which user can access it.
ii) A delegation can be made only if the user makes a request to the owner to access it.
iii) Users would be allowed to access a file even if the owner is not currently connected to the network.
iv) A delegation can be temporarily established from a user to a computing node.

4   Mutida Model

The Mutida method enables the management, delegation and revocation of file permissions. The goal is to allow the users to recreate all the file keys they have access to using a single local function and a key pair (each user possesses a private key pair $Kpriv_{User}$ and $Kpub_{User}$), with the assumption that the people we want to exchange with know the $Kpub_{User}$ value. Additionally, access to a piece of data must be possible even if the owner of this piece of data is not online. The solution also allows rights delegation to a third-party node for the execution of a specific task, such as data processing.

Our solution relies on a global ACL, similar to that of Wang et al. [58], which consists of key/value storage deployed in the same network. The values are public, and modifications are controlled by trusted nodes or consensus algorithms. This enables us to manage the file permissions without a centralized authority and even when the file owner is offline. We also rely on two local functions called $ID1$ and $ID2$, which are known by all the peers in the networks and will be detailed later in this section.

We summarize the assumptions of the Mutida protocol as follows:

i The files are stored in a public server and are publicly available.
ii Each file has a unique identifier: a unique filename or a UUID.
iii Each user has a secret key used as an input of the Mutida "ID" functions.
iv The ACL is centralized or distributed key/value storage. Records can be read by everybody, but modifications are not possible or are controlled by the key/value storage.
v The network exchanges are encrypted so that an adversary cannot intercept the messages and gain unauthorized access to files.

Figure 1 illustrates the network on which Mutida is deployed, with the IPFS storage system deployed at multiple locations and ACL nodes spread on each site. We assume that users connect to the closest node to store their files. As the main advantages of the Mutida approach in comparison with a standard approach, which consists of encrypting the file key with the public key of each user that wants access to the file, we can list the following:

i) Deleting a record in the ACL removes the access right for a user and for the computation nodes to which this right has been delegated. In a version using more traditional cryptography, this dependency is nonexistent.
ii) It is not possible to give access permission that a user has not requested. In Mutida, each delegation begins with the exchange of IDs that only the user receiving the delegation is able to calculate. In contrast, in a more "traditional" approach, knowing a user's public key is enough to create a record in the ACL, and therefore, grant rights. Although this can be overcome by using digital signatures, our approach integrates this functionality natively.
iii) For the performance of the RSA calculation or what Shamir compared to the additions of Mutida, in our case, the calculation is limited to a simple addition, whereas an asymmetric RSA-type encryption requires exponentiation. Quantitative data to justify this point are presented in Subsect. 6.1.

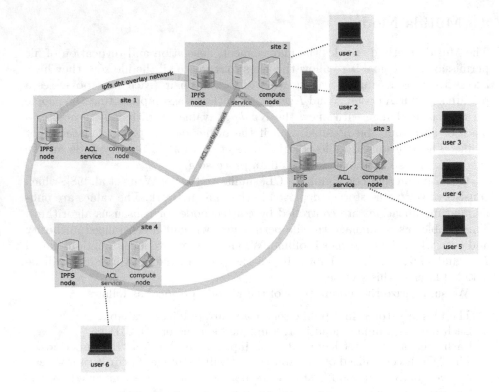

Fig. 1. Overview of the Mutida architecture.

iv) As a result of using a hash function, we have anonymity in the ACL; it is not possible from a record to determine which user and which file it corresponds to. In an approach using "classic" cryptography, there is no consensus to achieve such functionality.

4.1   Protocol Description

Hereafter, we describe the main operations, as shown in Fig. 2, that allow us to manage the file rights without a centralized authority and leverage from a distributed storage system. As the main requirements of the proposed protocol, we highlight the following:

i) The owner of a file chooses who can access it and delegates the right to selected users.
ii) The users that can access a piece of data can temporarily delegate their access rights to a computing node to execute some calculation.
iii) The owner should not be able to give to a user the permission to access a file if the user has not requested it.

iv) The allowed user should be able to access a file even if the owner is not currently connected to the network.
v) The revocation of access rights should also be available, even if not guaranteed, despite the nature of the storage solution.

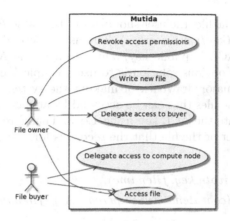

Fig. 2. Diagram of possible user actions in Mutida.

Writing a New File. Figure 3 shows the sequence diagram when a user wants to store a new file. The operation is divided into two phases. During the first phase, the user determines an encryption key and encrypts the file. The user selects a random value R_{owner}, denoted R in the diagram, and computes the key with the help of a previously agreed ID1 function, as the one described in Eq. 1. In the remainder of this text and equations, we refer to file identification as "filename" for simplicity, but for implementation purposes, a Universal Unique Identifier (UUID) of each file should be used.

Because the SHA256 function returns 256 bits, all the computations described below use binary words of that size. In other words, all the computations are modulo 2^{256}. This function is chosen due to its low collision probability and computing complexity, as we lack a correlation between the input and the output bits [18,45].

From the value computed in Eq. 1, the final value used as a key for the file would be according to Eq. 2.

$$ID1(user\_private\_key, filename)$$
$$= SHA256(concatenate(user\_private\_key, filename, "ID1")) \quad (1)$$

We note that in Eq. 1, the value ID1 between quotes corresponds to the actual word (it is not a recursive function). This string is used to create different

ID functions (ID1 and ID2) where the values are not correlated between them. These functions are easy to compute [48] by the user who knows the private key, though they appear completely random to others.

$$file\_decryption\_key = (ID1(owner\_private\_key, filename) + R_{owner}) \bmod 2^{256}$$

$$(2)$$

After encrypting the file, the user should store the value R_{owner} in the global and the public ACL (key/value storage). This is the second phase of the operation. Because the ACL is public key/value storage, the ACL key should be carefully chosen. The obvious solution is to use a couple ("user1", "file1"), but this couple has the major drawback of making the system transparent; every user can determine the files that can be accessed by anybody. To overcome this, we propose to compute the ACL key using Eq. 3. Therefore, an observer could not determine the user or the file that the record is for.

$$ID2(user\_private\_key, filename)$$
$$= SHA256(concatenate(user\_private\_key, filename, "ID2")) \qquad (3)$$

A signature is also added to the ACL record. It will enable the user to determine if the stored value has been modified or corrupted when it will be retrieved and allow verification of the user's the identity that created this record. The signature is not stored directly in the ACL because it can break the anonymity or the privacy of the user. Instead, we perform an XOR operation (noted $\oplus$) between the signature and the hash of the decryption key to ensure that only users who know the decryption key are able to extract the signature.

By computing the encryption key in the aforementioned way, we ensure that:

– If someone reads the public ACL and accesses the value R_{owner}, they cannot determine the decryption key because they cannot compute the value of $ID1(owner\_private\_key, filename)$ without the private key of the user.
– if someone reads the public ACL and knows the decryption key of a file (because it is allowed to), they cannot determine the private key of the user.
– If someone knows the value of $ID2(owner\_private\_key, filename)$, they cannot determine the key for the other files that the user can access.
– It is not necessary to keep a local keystore of all the files that the user has access to.

In Fig. 3, for illustrative purposes, we describe Eq. 1 as the function $ID1(owner\_private\_key, filename)$. In the figure, $user1(owner)$ creates a new ACL entry for $file1$ with the value 20, and the file encryption key would be the value 20 + 4497, where 4497 corresponds to their own $ID1$ value calculated using Eq. 1. Similarly, the computed value for the ACL using Eq. 3 is 2021.

Accessing a File as an Owner. The access of a file as an owner is illustrated in Fig. 4. The operation is divided into 4 phases: retrieving the value stored in the

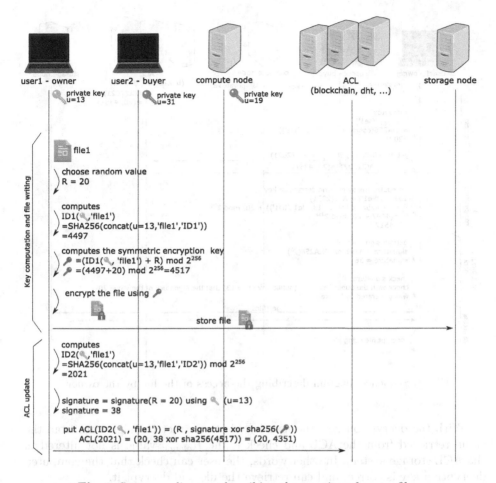

Fig. 3. Sequence diagram describing the creation of a new file.

ACL, computing the decryption key, checking the integrity of the value retrieved in the ACL, and finally, accessing the file and decrypting it.

To access the file, the user must first retrieve the value stored in the global ACL. The user first computes the value of the ACL key using $ID2(owner\_private\_key, filename) = 2021$. Afterward, the node retrieves the couple of values (Eq. 4) associated with the key.

$$R_{owner}, signature \oplus SHA256(key) \qquad (4)$$

With the value R_{owner}, the user computes the decryption key with the same formula as previously presented in Eq. 2. This allows us to recalculate all the keys for the files that we own or have access to without having to store any additional value locally. Once the user has recalculated the key, they only have to retrieve the file from the IPFS public storage and decrypt it.

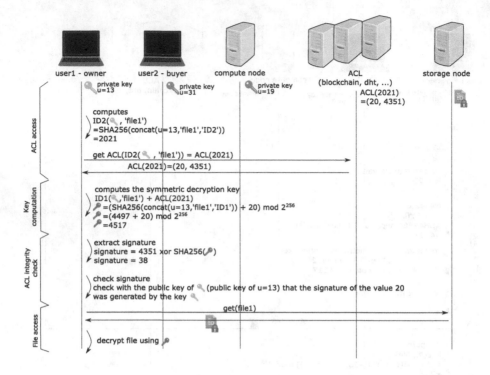

Fig. 4. Sequence diagram describing the access of the file by the owner.

With the decryption key, the user is able to extract the signature from the value retrieved from the ACL and check if the R_{owner} value is not altered in the ACL storage system. In other words, the user can check that the computed decryption key is correct and can retrieve the file and decrypt it.

In Fig. 4, $user1$ retrieves the previously stored value in ACL and is able to reconstruct the key just using this value and the value obtained by their $ID1$ function. The same would apply for multiple files, without the need to have a local keystore for each file that belongs to the user.

Access Delegation to Another User. The idea of the right delegation is to enable another user (called "buyer") to decrypt the file without re-encrypting it (we restate that IPFS stores immutable pieces of data). Therefore, the user who gains access to it will have to be able to compute the same decryption key as the owner, but using their own private key.

To accomplish that, the user has to request access to the data, as shown in the first phase of Fig. 5. The user uses Eq. 1 to compute a value that is then sent to the owner of the file. Because the value is sensitive, as it enables any malicious user who could learn it during the exchange to later be able to compute the decryption key, the user adds a random number (noted k) to it before sending it. In other words, the buyer sends the value ($ID1(buyer\_private\_key, filename) +$

k) mod 2^{256} to the owner of the file. The value k also enables the protocol to work in an asynchronous way by posting the request in a public queue that is processed once the owner of the file is online.

If the owner of the file agrees to give access, they retrieve the ACL value (second phase) and compute the delta+k value, which is the difference between the decryption key and the value sent by the buyer (3rd and 5th phases). The *delta* value is computed as in Eq. 5.

$$file\_decryption\_key = (ID1(buyer\_private\_key, filename) + k + delta) \ mod \ 2^{256} \tag{5}$$

In this computation, the owner cannot determine the private key of the user they give the permission to because of the use of a hashing function and the random value added to it. The value looks random to the owner, but it can be computed easily by the buyer. In the same way, the owner cannot use the value transmitted by the user to access the other files that this user is allowed to access because the $ID1$ value depends on the "filename" and the k value is unknown to the buyer. In the last two phases, the value *delta* is returned to the user who removes the random value k, as in Eqs. 6 and 7

$$R_{buyer} = (delta + k) \ mod \ 2^{256} \tag{6}$$

$$R_{buyer} = (file\_decryption\_key - ID1(buyer\_private\_key, filename) - k$$
$$+ k) \ mod \ 2^{256} \tag{7}$$

Finally, the user stores the value R_{buyer} in the ACL using the same mechanism as previously described, computes the key of the ACL record using the function $ID2$ and adds a signature to protect the record against any modification.

In Fig. 5, we illustrate the file access delegation process where $user2(buyer)$ sends a request to access $file1$ that belongs to $user1(owner)$, accompanied by their ID value (3951). To delegate the rights, $user1$ calculates a delta between the file decryption key and the ID1+k value of user 2 (561). $User2$ removes the k value and stores the R_{buyer} value (566) in a new ACL entry.

Accessing a File as a Delegated User. The user accesses the file using the same process previously described for the owner, where the single change is the value that is read corresponding to this user. The user has to read the value in the ACL, as in Eq. 8, and then compute the key with the same formula as previously presented, where $key = ID1(buyer\_private\_key, filename) + R_{buyer}$. Finally, the user can extract the signature, verify it and retrieve the file from the IPFS public storage before decrypting it

$$ACL(ID2(buyer\_private\_key, filename))$$
$$= (R_{buyer}, signature \oplus SHA256(decryption\_key)) \tag{8}$$

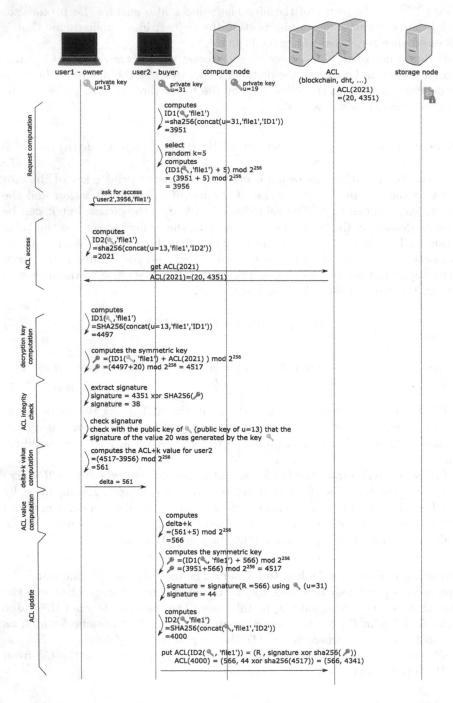

Fig. 5. Sequence diagram describing the rights delegation to a new user.

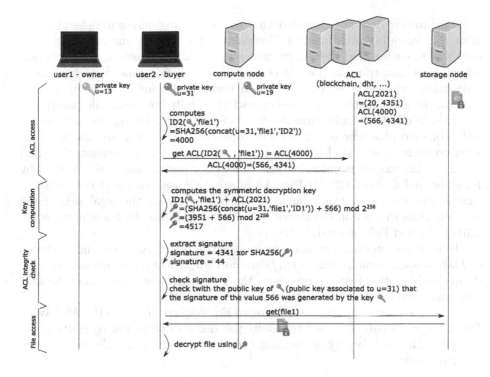

Fig. 6. Sequence diagram describing the access of the file by a delegated user.

In Fig. 6 we illustrate the file access by $user2$. The process starts by recovering the corresponding value in the ACL (566) and adding it to their own ID1 value (3951), which will result in the decryption key of $file1$ (4517).

Access Delegation to a Computing Node. A specificity of our approach is that a user can request a computing node to execute a software program that uses the user's data. The user can enable the computing node to access the pieces of data on their behalf to perform the requested computation.

The ideal approach would be to use fully homomorphic encryption [13] on the compute node so that the computation will be performed directly on the Encrypted pieces of data. However, due to the lack of maturity and the need for an operational solution, our delegation mechanism enables the node to compute the key and decrypt the pieces of data.

Delegating permission to a computing node is quite similar to delegating permission to a user. The difference is that instead of storing the value in the ACL, the user transmits it to the node directly. The idea is that the computing node does not need to access the files over a long period of time. The computing node can forget the value once the process requested by the user is terminated. Additionally, if at any moment there are changes in the permission for a given file, the same will be replicated for the computing node.

Our protocol does not guarantee that the computing node will delete the key after the computation is finished. However, to the best of our knowledge, the only way to ensure that there is no replica of the key is to utilize an encryption scheme that, according to Naehrig et al. (2011)) [44], is "somewhat" homomorphic, where we would support a limited number of homomorphic operations that can be much faster and more compact than fully homomorphic encryption schemes. While this could solve the issue of the user knowing the key, only a fully homomorphic scheme can prevent copies of the unencrypted file when we want to perform any kind of computation on it. Until this moment, this kind of encryption scheme is unfeasible due to its poor performance, as indicated by Fontaine and Galand (2011)) [20]. An alternative approach and the only one that seems feasible at the moment would be to rely on the legal side of the General Data Protection Regulation (GDPR) as proposed by Kieselmann et al. (2016) [33] and Politou et al. (2018) [46].

To start the process, the user requests the computing node to send the value of $ID1(compute\_node\_private\_key, filename) + k$, where k is a random number. As in the delegation between two users, the k value prevents any leak of the $ID1$ value and enables the protocol to work asynchronously.

Then, the user computes S according to Eq. 9, where R_{buyer} is the ACL value for the user. Finally, the user transmits the delta value to the compute node, as well as the ACL key by performing $ID2(user\_private\_key, filename)$ to the compute node.

$$S = decryption\_key - (ID1(compute\_node\_private\_key, filename) + k + R_{buyer})$$
$$(9)$$

In Fig. 7, we illustrate the rights delegation process from $user2$ to a computing node, where the computing node should use the same entry as the corresponding user. We start by asking for the ID of the respective computing node (5643) that is added to a random number k to protect the node against any leak of the ID1 value. Then, R_{buyer} is computed, which is obtained by the difference between the ID1 of $user2$ and the computing node's $ID1 + k$, obtaining (-1554).

Accessing a File from a Computing Node on Behalf of a User. To access a file, the computing node will read the ACL value of the user: R_{buyer}, then it computes Eq. 10, where S is the value transmitted by the user at the end of the delegation process. Because the node accesses the ACL value of user R_{buyer}, if the user has their access revoked and the ACL value is deleted, the computing node cannot compute the key and decrypt the files. We also note that the delegation is on a file basis. Therefore, the computing node cannot access all the files the user has access to.

$$file\_decryption\_key = ID1(compute\_node\_private\_key, filename)$$
$$+R_{buyer} + S + k \qquad (10)$$

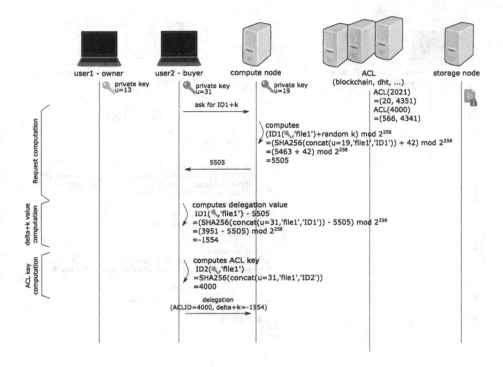

Fig. 7. Sequence diagram describing the delegation to a computing node.

In Fig. 8, we show the computing node utilizing the previously calculated R_{buyer}, as well as its own $ID1$ value and the one in the ACL to recalculate the file key. As in the previous scenarios, the node can verify that the value retrieved from the ACL has not been corrupted.

4.2 Storage of the Global ACL

The main characteristic of the ACL is being global and public. This means that each node should be able to access the values stored in it. The idea of using a public Access Control List is not new and it is used in different articles [2,37]. Several implementations can be evaluated to store this Access Control List, such as Distributed Hash Table (DHT), Blockchain, DNS and Gossip-based systems. Each of these solutions has some advantages and drawbacks. We attempt to evaluate them in the following sections.

Distributed Hash Table. A distributed hash table is a key/value data storage spread among several nodes. The nodes are organized around a virtual ring, and routing tables guarantee that each value can be retrieved by contacting at most $log(N)$ nodes (with N, the number of nodes). Different variants of distributed hash tables exist, such as Chord [55], Tapestry [63] and Kademlia [39], which attempt to optimize the routing process.

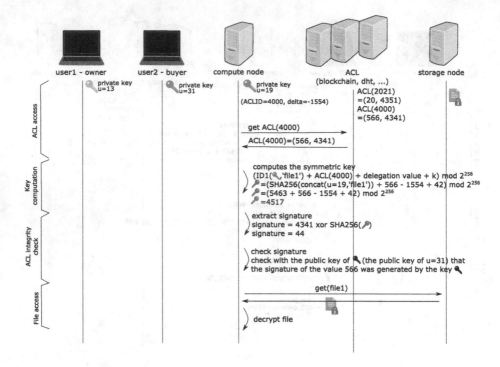

Fig. 8. Sequence diagram describing the access of the file by a computing node.

To store our ACL values, a DHT has many advantages. First, it guarantees that each value can be found by contacting a limited number of nodes, which leads to good performance. It also has the advantage of evenly spreading the values among all the nodes of the network. There is no node that stores more keys, and therefore, has more power to control the network.

However, there are two main drawbacks. The first is a classic drawback of a DHT; replication is not part of the protocol and should be managed on top of the DHT. Therefore, there is a risk that some keys are lost when nodes disconnect from the network. The other drawback is more important; a node that is responsible for storing a key can do everything with the key: it can delete it, modify the value or refuse to serve it to some nodes.

In other words, DHT does not natively support Byzantine faults and malicious nodes [57]. This is important for our protocol because if the owner of a certain file allows a second user to access it, a new key is inserted in the ACL. However, if the node storing this value does not let the user access it, it means that the ACL node has the power to limit the access beyond the will of the data owner.

Domain Name System. A domain name system [42] (DNS) is cused on the internet to associate IP addresses with domain names. The particularity of the protocol is to use a hierarchical namespace, such as "key.domain.".

This hierarchical organization leads to the spread of the workload and storage among different servers. This protocol has the same drawbacks as the distributed hash table (DHT), but it proposes a deterministic network routing. It also lacks automatic reconfiguration in the case of network modification [27]. For instance, when a node is added, an administrator has to create the DNS records to attach the new node in the tree. However, in the situation of ACL distribution, this protocol can be a solution in the case of some trusted nodes managing the top of the hierarchy, preventing users from being unable to access the records.

Blockchain. Another possible implementation for the key/value storing the ACL values is to use a public [61] or a private [5] blockchain. Blockchains are immutable data structures that work only as "append-only", which is replicated on all the nodes. Therefore, compared to a DHT, there is no risk that a user cannot retrieve a piece of data stored in it. In the situation of distributing the Access Control List, this property is important because it means that all of the nodes store a copy of it and no node is able to prevent any user from accessing it.

In addition to the data structure, blockchains provide a consensus algorithm. Each transaction is validated by a majority of nodes before being added to the blockchain. Therefore, any action of adding or modifying a value is not taken by one node in particular. The main drawback of a blockchain is the computing power to achieve a consensus. To overcome this, some proposals replace the consensus based on proof-of-work [61] with other types of proof, such as proof-of-stake [50] and proof-of-authority [6].

Another way to overcome this is to use a private blockchain. A private blockchain is one where nodes need the permission to participate. The nodes must be trusted and should not be malicious. The other disadvantage of blockchains is that no value can be deleted because of the append-only structure of the chain. Therefore, in our situation, it makes the revocation of access rights impossible.

Discussion. From the previous discussion, the choice to store the global ACL can be seen in the following order of preference:

i Blockchain is first because of its ability to make the ACL available across all nodes. It is also possible to deploy a hyperledger on all nodes that would manage ACLs in public transactions and handle the users who are allowed to join the network in a distributed way. Traceability can be managed by private transactions stored on trusted nodes.

ii DHT is next because of its ability to dynamically adapt to the network. Furthermore, this technology is already used in IPFS. We can imagine deploying this solution by inserting keys manually into the DHT of IPFS.

iii DNS is third because of its tree structure and performance. The root nodes of the tree can be managed by the trusted certifier nodes.

4.3   ACL Management

These different systems do not always provide strong consistency. Therefore, two simultaneous reads on the same record can lead to reading different values if the record was recently updated. This is particularly true in blockchains when new blocks have not been propagated to all the nodes or to the DNS when the zone was not updated on the secondary servers.

We believe this is not a real problem because there is a record for each user. Therefore, there are no concurrent reads between users. The second reason is that because data are immutable, ACL records do not vary much. For a user and a specific file, there are two possibilities: either the record is here and the user will be able to decrypt the file or the record is not here, which means that the user's right has been revoked.

In the worst scenario, the user that just received the permission cannot still decrypt the file or the user that just saw their permission revoked, though they can still access the file. There is no situation where the user computes the wrong key.

The second point is the security of the ACL. We previously described how a signature can help to determine if the record was tampered with, but it does not prevent tampering itself. There are two ways of managing this. If right revocation is not wanted, the ACL storage system can be a system in append-only mode. Therefore, no modification of the ACL is needed.

Otherwise, there must be a trust between the user and the ACL storage system that will need to verify some permissions. A simple way to manage the permission is to use a token that will be specified at the creation of a record and that must be given to delete it.

5   Methodology

An implementation of all the necessary Mutida components described in the previous sections is performed in Java Spring Boot. We rely on the standard MessageDigest library and $SHA - 256$ for the $ID(user, filename)$ function implementation. Each client is composed of a REST API with all the encryption, file and ACL endpoints, as well as an IPFS [49] peer for data storage. The platform is deployed using Kubernetes [56], where all the nodes allocated form a single cluster. This is illustrated in Fig. 9.

A single client is always hosted on the same physical node (co-located) using deployment constraints. The tests are carried out using the Gatling [22] software program, which sends requests to the aforementioned API. For all the propositions, the currently-implemented ACL mode is the replication mode, where a copy of the ACL's changes are sent in parallel to all nodes, and we wait for the responses in a synchronous way.

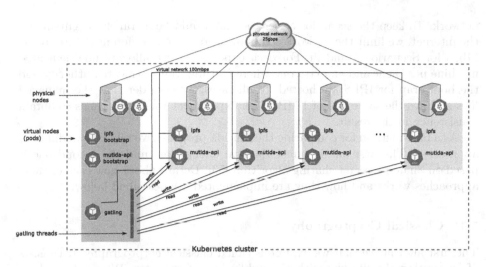

Fig. 9. Deployment of the solution in a Kubernetes cluster.

To evaluate the method, we propose three different scenarios: i) the first scenario entails evaluating the ACL without the impact of the data transfers and network exchanges, ii) the second scenario entails considering the network (i.e., data exchanged among different users) while keeping a uniform data access distribution, and iii) the third scenario is where we take a more realistic file distribution into consideration. In summary, we can describe the test scenarios as follows:

– **scenario i:** We encrypt data, create ACL entries, send files and access them locally, i.e., no data sharing with other users. The goal of this test is to evaluate the Mutida overhead in comparison with Shamir without the impact of the data sharing. In this scenario, 4 clients write n files; afterwards, the same 4 clients read them locally.
– **scenario ii:** We encrypt data, create ACL entries, send files, delegate rights to other users, and they access the files using the delegated values in the ACL. The goal of this test is to evaluate the total time impact that the Mutida approach would have in a complete scenario, including the data transaction. In this scenario, 4 clients write n files, and then 4 other clients read them.
– **scenario iii:** It is the same as scenario ii but follows a ZipF distribution [62] for files being accessed, where some files are more searched than others. The goals are the same as those from Scenario ii but rely on a more realistic file access distribution. In this scenario, n files are written on a single client and 3 different clients perform 100000 reads among these pieces of data.

These scenarios are evaluated in the "Gros" cluster of the Grid'5000 platform [9], located in Nancy, France. The cluster is composed of 124 Intel Xeon Gold 5220 18 cores/CPU, SSD storage and is interconnected with a 2×25 Gbps network. To keep the scenarios closer to what would be a transfer occurring on the internet, we limit the network communication among different clients to 100 Mbps for Scenarios ii and iii. For each experiment, we allocate one dedicated machine per client and an extra one where Gatling, the certificate authority and the bootstrap for IPFS are hosted. In all cases, we consider that the managed files all have the same size of 1 MB. Each experiment was run 5 times to obtain consistency in the results.

As a base method for comparing the Mutida proposal, we rely on two different approaches. The first one is called classical encryption, and the second one is based on Shamir's secret sharing algorithm [53]. Details about how each of these approaches works and how they are implemented are described below.

5.1 Classical Cryptography

The first alternative that we explore is called classical cryptography. It consists of encrypting the file key with the public key of the user. We want to share the file with and include it in the public ACL (instead of the $ID1$ approach previously presented and used by Mutida). The comparison with this approach is restricted only to a first set of tests, where we compare the performance of each operation. We opt to use Shamir as a base comparison method because its additional functionalities (previously detailed) are closer to those in Mutida's method.

5.2 The Base Comparison Method - Shamir's Secret Sharing

As a base method for comparing Mutida in the previously presented scenarios, we rely on Shamir's secret sharing algorithm [53], which is one of the classical methods to secure a secret in a distributed way. The algorithm consists of splitting an arbitrary secret S into N parts called shares, and then distributing them among different peers. Among N parts, we can affirm that at least K is necessary to reconstruct the original secret S. We use this algorithm to split the decryption key of the files into multiple parts that are kept by different nodes. This way of sharing a secret enables us to ensure that a single malicious peer will not be able to reconstruct the secret (given that $K > 1$). The CodeHale[1] implementation of Shamir's operations is the one used in the experiments.

In Fig. 10, the file is encrypted using a symmetric key. Then, the key is split into several parts that are spread among different ACL servers. The ACL servers also keep track of the users who are allowed to access the file. In Fig. 11, we show the process to read a file, where the user has to contact different servers. Each server independently checks the user's permission before sending the key part. Then, when enough key parts are retrieved, the user can reconstruct the key and decrypt the file. This method is used in the next section to evaluate the performance of the proposal even if the security provided is different.

---

[1] https://github.com/codahale/shamir.

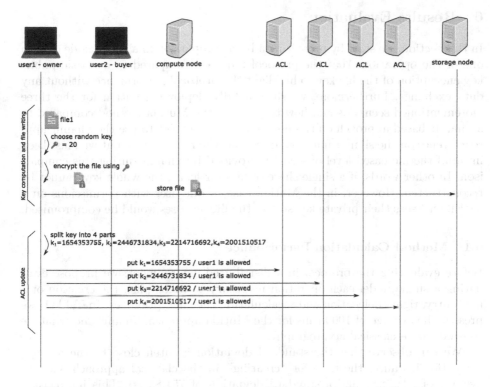

Fig. 10. Writing process using a protocol based on the Shamir algorithm.

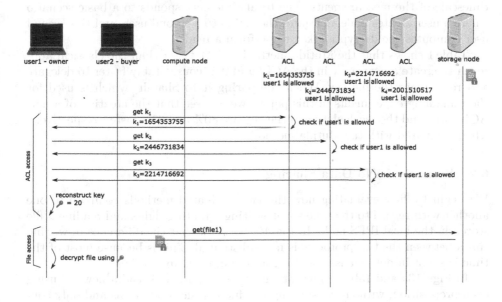

Fig. 11. Reading process using a protocol based on the Shamir algorithm.

6   Results Evaluation

In this section, we start by presenting a brief comparison in a single node of each one of the operations that the protocol requires, compared to a classic public key encryption of the file key to highlight the protocol performance without any data exchange. Furthermore, we show a fully deployed solution for the three aforementioned scenarios and how to perform the Mutida method compared to a Shamir-based approach on those scenarios. The choice to use the Shamir approach relies on the similar functionalities that the method has, but we must keep in mind the increased level of security provided by Shamir during this comparison. In other words, if a single share of Shamir leaks, the whole key cannot be reconstructed. However, in the Mutida case, if one user with permissions on a specific file sees their private key stolen, the file accesses would be compromised.

6.1   Method Calculation Performance

Before evaluating the protocol in a distributed environment, we propose evaluating a single node, each operation necessary to accomplish the creation of a new entry, rights delegation and recalculating the encryption key. In Table 1, we present the average of 1000 runs for the Mutida approach, Shamir and what we consider to be classical cryptography.

We can observe that the standard deviation is often close to the average value (for instance, the time for "creating" in the classical approach with an average of $123.78\,\mu s$ and a standard deviation of $751.83\,\mu s$). This imprecision of the measure is due to the process scheduler of the operating system and the timescale of the measurements. The total time corresponds to a basic scenario where a user creates a file, delegates the rights to a second user, and this second user computes the decryption key to perform a read.

Table 1 shows that the Mutida method is 57% faster than the classical approach to create a new entry in the ACL, and it is considerably faster to delegate and recalculate the file key. When comparing it to Shamir, which is used for the remaining experiments in this paper, we can see that the creation of a new ACL entry and the recalculation of the key are 80% and 97% faster, respectively, when compared with the Mutida method.

6.2   Scenario I: No Data Sharing

We begin by first evaluating how the two evaluated methods compare to one another with regard to the time spent writing, granting rights and reading a file stored in the local IPFS node. In Fig. 12, we show that the difference in writing times between the two protocols is not substantial. This is because most of the time is spent in data transfer and i/o access in both approaches.

In Figs. 13a and 13b, we present the time to write and read a new file using each proposition, without considering the file transfer operations and only considering the ones concerning the ACL and rights management operations. The operations that are considered in each case are described below.

Table 1. Time comparison of each operation for the Mutida, Shamir and classic cryptography

Operation	Mutida		Classical		Shamir	
			Time (μs)			
	Avg	Stdev	Avg	Stdev	Avg	Stdev
Create	**53.02**	97.28	123.78	751.83	272.06	199.23
Delegate	**10.05**	31.91	1770.82	382.11	N/A	N/A
Recalculate	**10.57**	44.19	1677.20	317.32	424.89	368.61
Total	73.64		3571.8		696.95	

When considering the protocol based on Shamir's method, the operations are (i) splitting the key, (ii) distribution of the parts on the different nodes, and (iii) encryption of the file. For reading, the operations are (i) retrieval of the key parts from the nodes, (ii) reconstruction of the key, and (iii) decryption of the file.

For Mutida's method, the operations considered for writing are (i) choosing a random number K for the ACL, (ii) computing the value of $SHA256(private\_key, filename) + K$, (iii) Storing the value K in the distributed ACL (on the different nodes), and (iv) Encryption of the file. For reading, the operations are (i) Computing the value of $SHA256(private\_key, filename) + K$ and (ii) Decryption of the file. We note that the ACL values and the key parts are spread in a synchronous way.

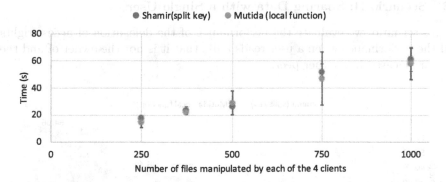

Fig. 12. Time for each client to encrypt {250,500,750,1000} files, to write them on their local server and to spread the key parts (Shamir) or the ACL value in the nodes.

Figures 13a and 13b show the access rights operations for the two solutions. It is between 5–10 seconds in writing and less than 1 s while reading. This is an important result because it means that when data are not shared, adding a protocol to manage access rights does not impact the performance.

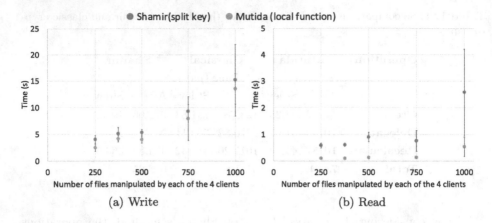

Fig. 13. Overhead of time due to the access right management.

In writing, our proposal has the same overhead as Shamir's solution because in the two approaches, ACL values need to be spread to all nodes. This network exchange is the operation that takes the most time and has more of an impact on the overhead. However, during the reading process, our approach has a lower overhead than the approach relying on a splitting key. This is because in our approach, the node only has to perform local operations (retrieving the ACL value and computing the ID ($ID(private\_key, filename)$ value), but in the Shamir approach, the node has to contact other nodes to retrieve the key parts.

6.3 Scenario II: Sharing Data with a Single User

In this scenario, we evaluate the performance of the delegation of access rights and the performance when a user reads a file that it is not the owner of and the data are located in another peer.

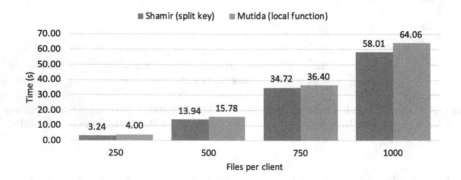

Fig. 14. Time to delegate the rights for the readers

Delegation of the Access Rights to the Readers. With regard to Shamir, the delegation consists of sending a request to the node that has previously written the file. The node propagates the request to all the nodes to ensure that they can record the fact that the reader is allowed to retrieve the key parts. In Mutida, the delegation is the protocol presented in Sect. 4. It consists of the reader computing the value ID $ID(private\_key, filename)$ and transmitting it to the node that wrote the file. The node computes the ACL value using its own private key and propagates this ACL value to all nodes that store it.

In the two propositions, we consider the time to realize the propagation to all the nodes. The main difference is that in our proposal, we have an extra exchange because the user has to compute a value that is transmitted to the file owner. Then, the file owner performs the propagation of the ACL value. This process is confirmed in Fig. 14, which shows that the time to delegate access rights is more important with Mutida and is linear with the number of files.

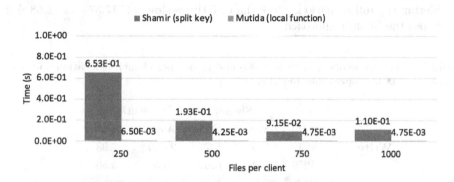

Fig. 15. Time to get the key to decrypt the file.

Reading of the Files. Fig. 15 shows the amount of time that is required to obtain the key needed to decrypt the file using 4 clients. In Shamir, it corresponds to the time to obtain the key parts from other nodes and the time to execute the Shamir reconstruction algorithm. In Mutida, it is the time to compute $ID(private\_key, filename)$ and to add it to the local value of the ACL.

Despite the less time that rights delegation and key recalculation might take in comparison with data transfer and more costly network operations, this is still an important time and cost saving improvement.

6.4 Scenario III: Real-World Use Case

In this scenario, each client writes 1000 files. Then, among all the files that have been written, each client generates 100,000 read requests using a zipf function ($skew = 0.5$). The zipf function represents the workload of a "real world" application [12,62]. The delegation of access rights is performed during the first read, only once per couple (client, file). Then, only read operations are performed. The clients do not store the decryption key of the file recently read and reconstruct the key for each access.

Table 2 shows that in writing, Mutida is slightly slower than Shamir, but as shown by the standard deviation, this is not because Mutida is fundamentally slower; it is because of a lack of consistency in the test execution. Table 2 also shows that the approach using Mutida takes 8 times longer (1.23 s vs 0.16 s) to delegate access rights than the approach using Shamir due to the calculation of the ID by the buyer and its transfer to the node of the owner.

However, this extra time is compensated by the different reads, since the time spent to recover the key parts needed by Shamir amount on average to 719.24 s compared to the 4.39 s spent by Mutida. Because some files are read several times but access delegation needs to be performed once, the total access time is shorter in the Mutida version than in the Shamir version when considering the full interaction of write, delegation and read. The average difference when considering the full scenario is more than 17 times slower (747.37 s vs 41.68 s) if we choose the Shamir approach.

Table 2. Time (in seconds) of write (1000 operations per client), delegation and read operations (100 000 operations per client).

		Shamir		Mutida	
		Average	**Stdev**	**Average**	**Stdev**
Write	ACL	12.03	5.77	24.60	7.98
	IPFS	15.54	6.62	10.50	3.89
	Total	27.57	8.82	35.10	10.96
Delegation		0.16	0.06	1.23	0.51
Read	ACL	**719.24**	141.68	**4.39**	9.15
	IPFS	0.40	0.14	0.96	0.17
	Total	719.64	141.62	5.35	9.47
Total		**747.37**		**41.68**	

6.5 Discussion of Results

The conducted experiments show that the amount of time to manage access rights and reconstruct the decryption keys is very small, leading to a small overhead. We start by highlighting that the Mutida method has a better performance when compared to classic cryptography, as well as when compared to Shamir's method. It requires less computational resources and has useful features, such as the impossibility of delegating access rights to a user who did not request it, as well as the possibility of giving temporary access to a computing node without adding a permanent record in the ACL.

Our first tests show that the most important overhead is not related to the computation but is due to the network traffic spreading ACL records between nodes. Further results show that Shamir and Mutida have a similar performance in writing a new entry because they execute similar operations, including generating a random key and propagating the ACL across all nodes. We also observe that Mutida has a considerably better performance in reading and reconstructing the file key. This is because the ACL is replicated on all the nodes, so Mutida is able to compute the decryption key without any network exchange, in contrast to Shamir, where all the key shares need to be recovered from the other peers. Soliciting fewer of the other nodes means that it allows them fewer possibilities to act maliciously.

One of the main drawbacks observed in the method is related to rights revocation, but in this specific structure, it would be the same for all the current approaches. The difficulty of revoking the rights is related to the storage method for the ACL records and the use of immutable pieces of data rather than a weakness in the right management protocol.

Finally, we are also able to observe that the largest overhead of the whole process is related to the file transfer itself. Even if in this first moment we focus on the delegation mechanisms of Mutida, its performance compared to other methods from the literature, as well as the additional functionalities and the anonymization of the rights management, this overhead can make Mutida suitable for IoT environments that use files of only a few kilobytes [43].

7 Conclusion

In this paper, we introduce Mutida, a protocol to manage access rights in a distributed storage solution, which allows us to delegate these rights to other users and compute the nodes.

In comparison to standard approaches, Mutida differs in the following aspects: (i) Mutida has the ability to distrust the storage nodes to manage access rights; (ii) it has a low computational cost; (iii) it has low requirements for the users that only have to store their key to be able to decrypt all the pieces of data they can access; (iv) it has the ability to delegate access rights to users and compute nodes; and (v) it has the ability to remove the rights of compute nodes when the access rights of the user have been revoked. Additionally, we can use our approach coupled with a distributed P2P storage system allowing us to access the files even when the user is disconnected, without having to rely on them in a centralized server.

We begin by showing the time spent on each individual operation of the Mutida method compared with Shamir and the classical Public Key Cryptography, where Mutida takes almost half of the time in comparison with these other methods. After we present a quantitative analysis between the Mutida and Shamir approaches considering three different scenarios, the first scenario is without data sharing, where we can clearly see the overhead of Shamir, especially when we want to read a file. After the second and third scenarios where the data exchange takes place, we see, especially in scenario iii, the difference in the total time of the file exchange when comparing the two methods, where Shamir can be up to 17 times slower than Mutida.

As limitations of the protocol, because data are stored in an immutable and distributed way and despite the rights revocation, there is no way to ensure that there is no copy of the data stored and that a malicious user that once had access at some point did not store the keys; the revocation is not guaranteed. Finally, we aim to continue this work by performing a detailed security analysis of the proposed mechanism and evaluating the long-term effects of this proposition in a production environment.

Acknowledgements. Experiments presented in this paper were carried out using the Grid'5000 testbed, supported by a scientific interest group hosted by Inria and including CNRS, RENATER and several Universities as well as other organizations (see https://www.grid5000.fr).

References

1. Adya, A., et al.: Farsite: federated, available, and reliable storage for an incompletely trusted environment. SIGOPS Oper. Syst. Rev. **36**(SI), 1–14 (2003). https://doi.org/10.1145/844128.844130
2. Ali, G., Ahmad, N., Cao, Y., Asif, M., Cruickshank, H., Ali, Q.E.: Blockchain based permission delegation and access control in internet of things (BACI). Comput. Secur. **86**, 318–334 (2019). https://doi.org/10.1016/j.cose.2019.06.010
3. Ali, M., et al.: SeDaSC: secure data sharing in clouds. IEEE Syst. J. **11**(2), 395–404 (2017). https://doi.org/10.1109/JSYST.2014.2379646
4. Andersen, M.P., et al.: WAVE: a decentralized authorization framework with transitive delegation. In: Proceedings of the 28th USENIX Conference on Security Symposium, pp. 1375–1392. SEC 2019, USENIX Association, USA (2019)
5. Androulaki, E., et al.: Hyperledger fabric: a distributed operating system for permissioned blockchains. In: Proceedings of the Thirteenth EuroSys Conference. EuroSys 2018, Association for Computing Machinery, NY (2018). https://doi.org/10.1145/3190508.3190538
6. Angelis, S.D., Aniello, L., Baldoni, R., Lombardi, F., Margheri, A., Sassone, V.: PBFT vs proof-of-authority: applying the CAP theorem to permissioned blockchain. In: Italian Conference on Cyber Security(2018). https://eprints.soton.ac.uk/415083/
7. Aura, T.: Distributed access-rights management with delegation certificates. In: Vitek, J., Jensen, C.D. (eds.) Secure Internet Programming. LNCS, vol. 1603, pp. 211–235. Springer, Heidelberg (1999). https://doi.org/10.1007/3-540-48749-2_9
8. Backes, M., Camenisch, J., Sommer, D.: Anonymous yet accountable access control. In: Proceedings of the 2005 ACM Workshop on Privacy in the Electronic Society, pp. 40–46. WPES 2005, Association for Computing Machinery, NY (2005). https://doi.org/10.1145/1102199.1102208
9. Balouek, D., et al.: Adding virtualization capabilities to the Grid'5000 testbed. In: Ivanov, I.I., van Sinderen, M., Leymann, F., Shan, T. (eds.) CLOSER 2012. CCIS, vol. 367, pp. 3–20. Springer, Cham (2013). https://doi.org/10.1007/978-3-319-04519-1_1

10. Battah, A.A., Madine, M.M., Alzaabi, H., Yaqoob, I., Salah, K., Jayaraman, R.: Blockchain-based multi-party authorization for accessing IPFS encrypted data. IEEE Access **8**, 196813–196825 (2020). https://doi.org/10.1109/ACCESS.2020. 3034260
11. Benet, J.: IPFS - Content Addressed, Versioned, P2P File System. Tech. rep., Protocol Labs, Inc. (2014). http://arxiv.org/abs/1407.3561
12. Breslau, L., Cao, P., Fan, L., Phillips, G., Shenker, S.: Web caching and Zipf-like distributions: evidence and implications. In: IEEE INFOCOM 1999. Conference on Computer Communications. Proceedings. Eighteenth Annual Joint Conference of the IEEE Computer and Communications Societies. The Future is Now (Cat. No. 99CH36320), vol. 1, pp. 126–134 (1999). https://doi.org/10.1109/INFCOM.1999. 749260
13. Chaudhary, P., Gupta, R., Singh, A., Majumder, P.: Analysis and comparison of various fully homomorphic encryption techniques. In: 2019 International Conference on Computing, Power and Communication Technologies (GUCON), pp. 58–62 (2019)
14. Chen, J., Ma, H.: Efficient decentralized attribute-based access control for cloud storage with user revocation. In: 2014 IEEE International Conference on Communications (ICC), pp. 3782–3787 (2014). https://doi.org/10.1109/ICC.2014.6883910
15. Chow, S.S.M., Weng, J., Yang, Y., Deng, R.H.: Efficient unidirectional proxy re-encryption. In: Bernstein, D.J., Lange, T. (eds.) AFRICACRYPT 2010. LNCS, vol. 6055, pp. 316–332. Springer, Heidelberg (2010). https://doi.org/10.1007/978-3-642-12678-9_19
16. Chuat, L., Abdou, A., Sasse, R., Sprenger, C., Basin, D., Perrig, A.: SoK: delegation and revocation, the missing links in the web's chain of trust. In: 2020 IEEE European Symposium on Security and Privacy (EuroS P), pp. 624–638 (2020). https://doi.org/10.1109/EuroSP48549.2020.00046
17. Crampton, J., Khambhammettu, H.: Delegation in role-based access control. Int. J. Inf. Secur. **7**, 123–136 (2008). https://doi.org/10.1007/s10207-007-0044-8
18. Dang, Q.: Secure hash standard (2015). https://doi.org/10.6028/NIST.FIPS.180-4
19. Daswani, N., Garcia-Molina, H., Yang, B.: Open problems in data-sharing peer-to-peer systems. In: Calvanese, D., Lenzerini, M., Motwani, R. (eds.) ICDT 2003. LNCS, vol. 2572, pp. 1–15. Springer, Heidelberg (2003). https://doi.org/10.1007/3-540-36285-1_1
20. Fontaine, C., Galand, F.: A survey of homomorphic encryption for nonspecialists. EURASIP J. Inf. Secur. **2007**, 013801 (2007). https://doi.org/10.1155/2007/13801
21. Gasser, M., McDermott, E.: An architecture for practical delegation in a distributed system. In: 2012 IEEE Symposium on Security and Privacy, p. 20. IEEE Computer Society, Los Alamitos, CA (1990). https://doi.org/10.1109/RISP.1990. 63835
22. Gatling Corp: Gatling (2021). https://gatling.io/. Accessed 28 June 2021
23. Gengler, B.: Content protection for recordable media (CPRM). Comput. Fraud Secur. **2001**(2), 5–6 (2001). https://doi.org/10.1016/S1361-3723(01)02011-5
24. Hardt, D., et al.: The OAuth 2.0 authorization framework (2012)
25. Heckmann, O., Bock, A., Mauthe, A., Steinmetz, R.: The eDonkey file-sharing network. In: Dadam, P., Reichert, M. (eds.) Informatik 2004, Informatik verbindet, Band 2, Beiträge der 34. Jahrestagung der Gesellschaft für Informatik e.V. (GI), pp. 224–228. Gesellschaft für Informatik e.V., Bonn (2004)
26. Henningsen, S., Rust, S., Florian, M., Scheuermann, B.: Crawling the IPFS network. In: 2020 IFIP Networking Conference (Networking), pp. 679–680 (2020)

27. Hesselman, C., Moura, G.C., De Oliveira Schmidt, R., Toet, C.: Increasing DNS security and stability through a control plane for top-level domain operators. IEEE Commun. Mag. **55**(1), 197–203 (2017). https://doi.org/10.1109/MCOM. 2017.1600521CM
28. Tran, H., Hitchens, M., Varadharajan, V., Watters, P.: A trust based access control framework for P2P file-sharing systems. In: Proceedings of the 38th Annual Hawaii International Conference on System Sciences, p. 302c (2005)
29. Jawad, M., Alvarado, P.S., Valduriez, P.: Design of PriServ, a privacy service for DHTs. In: Proceedings of the 2008 International Workshop on Privacy and Anonymity in Information Society, pp. 21–25. PAIS 2008, Association for Computing Machinery, NY (2008). https://doi.org/10.1145/1379287.1379293
30. Jin, H., Lotspiech, J.: Broadcast encryption for differently privileged. In: Gritzalis, D., Lopez, J. (eds.) SEC 2009. IAICT, vol. 297, pp. 283–293. Springer, Heidelberg (2009). https://doi.org/10.1007/978-3-642-01244-0_25
31. Katzarova, M., Simpson, A.: Delegation in a distributed healthcare context: a survey of current approaches. In: Katsikas, S.K., López, J., Backes, M., Gritzalis, S., Preneel, B. (eds.) ISC 2006. LNCS, vol. 4176, pp. 517–529. Springer, Heidelberg (2006). https://doi.org/10.1007/11836810_37
32. Kaushik, S., Gandhi, C.: Capability based outsourced data access control with assured file deletion and efficient revocation with trust factor in cloud computing. Int. J. Cloud Appl. Comput. **10**(1), 64–84 (2020). https://doi.org/10.4018/IJCAC. 2020010105
33. Kieselmann, O., Kopal, N., Wacker, A.: A novel approach to data revocation on the internet. In: Garcia-Alfaro, J., Navarro-Arribas, G., Aldini, A., Martinelli, F., Suri, N. (eds.) DPM/QASA -2015. LNCS, vol. 9481, pp. 134–149. Springer, Cham (2016). https://doi.org/10.1007/978-3-319-29883-2_9
34. Lasla, N., Younis, M., Znaidi, W., Ben Arbia, D.: Efficient distributed admission and revocation using blockchain for cooperative its. In: 2018 9th IFIP International Conference on New Technologies, Mobility and Security (NTMS), pp. 1–5 (2018). https://doi.org/10.1109/NTMS.2018.8328734
35. Legout, A., Urvoy-Keller, G., Michiardi, P.: Understanding BitTorrent: an experimental perspective. Technical report, Inria (2005). https://hal.inria.fr/inria-00000156
36. Lesueur, F., Me, L., Tong, V.V.T.: An efficient distributed PKI for structured P2P networks. In: 2009 IEEE Ninth International Conference on Peer-to-Peer Computing, pp. 1–10 (2009)
37. Liu, J., Li, X., Ye, L., Zhang, H., Du, X., Guizani, M.: BPDS: a blockchain based privacy-preserving data sharing for electronic medical records. In: 2018 IEEE Global Communications Conference (GLOBECOM), pp. 1–6 (2018)
38. Manousakis, K., et al.: Torrent-based dissemination in infrastructure-less wireless networks. J. Cyber Secur. Mobil. **4**(1), 1–22 (2015)
39. Maymounkov, P., Mazières, D.: Kademlia: a peer-to-peer information system based on the XOR metric. In: Druschel, P., Kaashoek, F., Rowstron, A. (eds.) IPTPS 2002. LNCS, vol. 2429, pp. 53–65. Springer, Heidelberg (2002). https://doi.org/10. 1007/3-540-45748-8_5
40. Merkle, R.C.: Protocols for public key cryptosystems. In: 1980 IEEE Symposium on Security and Privacy, p. 122 (1980). https://doi.org/10.1109/SP.1980.10006
41. Miller, S.P., Neuman, B.C., Schiller, J.I., Saltzer, J.H.: Kerberos authentication and authorization system. In: In Project Athena Technical Plan (1988)
42. Mockapetris, P.: Domain names - concepts and facilities. RFC 1034 (1987). https:// doi.org/10.17487/RFC1034

43. Muralidharan, S., Ko, H.: An InterPlanetary file system (IPFS) based IoT framework. In: 2019 IEEE International Conference on Consumer Electronics (ICCE), pp. 1–2 (2019). https://doi.org/10.1109/ICCE.2019.8662002
44. Naehrig, M., Lauter, K., Vaikuntanathan, V.: Can homomorphic encryption be practical? In: Proceedings of the 3rd ACM Workshop on Cloud Computing Security Workshop, pp. 113–124. CCSW 2011, Association for Computing Machinery, NY (2011). https://doi.org/10.1145/2046660.2046682
45. Nakatani, Y.: Structured allocation-based consistent hashing with improved balancing for cloud infrastructure. IEEE Trans. Parallel Distrib. Syst. 32(9), 2248–2261 (2021). https://doi.org/10.1109/TPDS.2021.3058963
46. Politou, E., Alepis, E., Patsakis, C.: Forgetting personal data and revoking consent under the GDPR: challenges and proposed solutions. J. Cybersecur. 4(1), tyy001 (2018). https://doi.org/10.1093/cybsec/tyy001
47. Politou, E., Alepis, E., Patsakis, C., Casino, F., Alazab, M.: Delegated content erasure in IPFS. Future Gener. Comput. Syst. 112, 956–964 (2020). https://doi.org/10.1016/j.future.2020.06.037
48. Preneel, B.: Cryptographic hash functions. Eur. Trans. Telecommun. 5(4), 431–448 (1994)
49. Protocol Labs: IPFS (2021). https://ipfs.io/. Accessed 28 June 2021
50. Saleh, F.: Blockchain without waste: proof-of-stake. Rev. Financ. Stud. 34(3), 1156–1190 (2020). https://doi.org/10.1093/rfs/hhaa075
51. Sari, L., Sipos, M.: FileTribe: blockchain-based secure file sharing on IPFS. In: European Wireless 2019; 25th European Wireless Conference, pp. 1–6 (2019)
52. Schnitzler, T., Dürmuth, M., Pöpper, C.: Towards contractual agreements for revocation of online data. In: Dhillon, G., Karlsson, F., Hedström, K., Zúquete, A. (eds.) SEC 2019. IAICT, vol. 562, pp. 374–387. Springer, Cham (2019). https://doi.org/10.1007/978-3-030-22312-0_26
53. Shamir, A.: How to share a secret. Commun. ACM 22(11), 612–613 (1979). https://doi.org/10.1145/359168.359176
54. Steichen, M., Fiz, B., Norvill, R., Shbair, W., State, R.: Blockchain-based, decentralized access control for IPFS. In: 2018 IEEE International Conference on Internet of Things (iThings) and IEEE Green Computing and Communications (GreenCom) and IEEE Cyber, Physical and Social Computing (CPSCom) and IEEE Smart Data (SmartData), pp. 1499–1506 (2018)
55. Stoica, I., et al.: Chord: a scalable peer-to-peer lookup protocol for internet applications. IEEE ACM Trans. Netw. 11(1), 17–32 (2003). https://doi.org/10.1109/TNET.2002.808407
56. The Linux Foundation: Kubernetes (2021). https://kubernetes.io/. Accessed 28 June 2021
57. Urdaneta, G., Pierre, G., Steen, M.V.: A survey of DHT security techniques. ACM Comput. Surv. 43(2), 1–49 (2011). https://doi.org/10.1145/1883612.1883615
58. Wang, S., Zhang, Y., Zhang, Y.: A blockchain-based framework for data sharing with fine-grained access control in decentralized storage systems. IEEE Access 6, 38437–38450 (2018)
59. Wang, X., Sun, X., Sun, G., Luo, D.: CST: P2P anonymous authentication system based on collaboration signature. In: 2010 5th International Conference on Future Information Technology, pp. 1–7 (2010). https://doi.org/10.1109/FUTURETECH.2010.5482740
60. Xu, R., Chen, Y., Blasch, E., Chen, G.: BlendCAC: a smart contract enabled decentralized capability-based access control mechanism for the IoT. Computers 7(3), 39 (2018). https://doi.org/10.3390/computers7030039

61. Yang, W., Garg, S., Raza, A., Herbert, D., Kang, B.: Blockchain: trends and future. In: Yoshida, K., Lee, M. (eds.) PKAW 2018. LNCS (LNAI), vol. 11016, pp. 201–210. Springer, Cham (2018). https://doi.org/10.1007/978-3-319-97289-3_15
62. Yang, Y., Zhu, J.: Write Skew and Zipf distribution: evidence and implications. ACM Trans. Storage **12**(4), 1–19 (2016). https://doi.org/10.1145/2908557
63. Zhao, B., Huang, L., Stribling, J., Rhea, S., Joseph, A., Kubiatowicz, J.: Tapestry: a resilient global-scale overlay for service deployment. IEEE J. Sel. Areas Commun. **22**(1), 41–53 (2004). https://doi.org/10.1109/JSAC.2003.818784

OpenCEMS: An Open Solution for Easy Data Management in Connected Environments

Richard Chbeir[1]([envelope]), Elio Mansour[2], Sabri Allani[1], Taoufik Yeferny[1],
Jean-Raphael Richa[1], Farid Yessoufou[1], and Sana Sellami[3]

[1] Univ Pau & Pays Adour, E2S-UPPA, LIUPPA, 3000 Anglet, France
{richard.chbeir,sabri.allani,taoufik.yeferny,jean-raphael.richa,
farid.yessoufou}@univ-pau.fr
[2] Scient Analytics, Paris, France
elio.mansour@scient.io
[3] Aix-Marseille Univ, Université de Toulon, CNRS, LIS, Laboratoire d'Informatique
et Systèmes, 7020 Marseille, France
sana.sellami@univ-amu.fr

Abstract. Automating the life cycle of data management projects is a challenging issue that has attracted the interest of both academic researchers and industrial companies. Therefore, several commercial and academic tools have been proposed to be used in a broad range of contexts. However, when dealing with data generated from connected environments (e.g., smart homes, cities), the data acquisition and management becomes more complex and heavily dependant on the environmental context thus rendering traditional tools less efficient and appropriate. In this respect, we introduce here OpenCEMS, an open platform for data management and analytics that can be used in various application domains and contexts, and more specifically in designing connected environments and analysing their generated/simulated data. Indeed, OpenCEMS provides a wide array of functionalities ranging from data pre-processing to post-processing allowing to represent and manage data from the different components of a connected environment (e.g., hardware, software) and to define the interactions between them. This allows to both simulate data with respect to different parameters as well as to contextualise collected data from the connected devices (i.e., consider environmental/sensing contexts). In this paper, we compare OpenCEMS with existing solutions and show how data is represented and processed.

Keywords: Data analytics · Connected environments

Supported by OpenCEMS Industrial Chair.

A. Hameurlain and A. M. Tjoa (Eds.): *Transactions on Large-Scale Data- and Knowledge-Centered Systems LII*, LNCS 13470, pp. 35–69, 2022.
https://doi.org/10.1007/978-3-662-66146-8_2

1   Introduction

In the last few years, advances in sensing, computing and networking technologies have contributed to the great success of Connected Environments (CEs), such as, smart homes, smart buildings, Intelligent Transportation Systems (ITS) [3,4,22]. Indeed, a variety of CE applications have been introduced in several sectors and have succeeded in providing a lot of benefits to the CE stakeholders and their end-users. The analysis of raw data generated from the connected devices plays a central role in the success and the growth of the CE applications, which brings data analytics into the picture. In fact, examining the collected CE data through the suitable data analytics processes allows to extract meaningful conclusions and actionable insights. These conclusions are usually in the form of trends, patterns, and statistics that aid business organizations in proactively engaging with data to implement effective decision-making processes. According to the Cross Industry Standard Process for Data Mining, known as the CRISP-DM methodology, a typical data analytics project includes the following six phases: (i) Business Understanding; (ii) Data Understanding; (iii) Data Preparation; (iv) Modelling; (v) Evaluation; and (vi) Deployment. It is worth mentioning that each phase involves different tasks. Furthermore, in practice, these phases can be performed in a different order and it will often be necessary to backtrack to previous phases and repeat certain tasks. Automating the life cycle of data analytics projects is a challenging issue that has attracted the interest of both academic researchers and industrial companies. In this respect, several commercial and academic tools have been proposed and can classified into two categories: Network-oriented and Data-oriented. Network-oriented solutions allow to manage IoT and connected devices. Network-oriented solutions offer various interesting functionalities (network mapping, IoT Device Maintenance, monitoring, intrusion detection, Endpoint Management, etc.), but they are limited in terms of data processing to help stack holders take insightful decisions. Data-oriented solutions have been currently designed to be generically used regardless of the data source, the data acquiring context, and the data feature particularities. Some of them are academic [2,14,16,26,32,35] while others are industrial (e.g., BigQuery[1], Watson Studio[2], Amazon AWS[3], Azure Analysis Services[4]). Although these solutions provide coverage for various use cases, they are not fully adapted to connected environment specifics and suffer from the following limitations: i) lack of an adequate representation of connected environment components (e.g., modeling infrastructures, devices, sensors, sensor observations, and the application domain); ii) no consideration of device specifics and their impact on the availability and quality of data (e.g., device mobility impact, device breakdown impact, sensing context impact); and iii) lack of consideration of the application domain (e.g., medical, energy management, environmental applications).

---

[1] https://cloud.google.com/bigquery.
[2] https://www.ibm.com/cloud.
[3] https://aws.amazon.com/.
[4] https://azure.microsoft.com/.

To overcome these limitations, we introduce here a hybrid solution called Connected Environment & Distributed Energy Data Management Solutions (OpenCEMS), an open platform for data management and analytics that can be used in various application domains and contexts (e.g., energy management in smart buildings, pollution monitoring in smart cities), and more specifically in designing CEs and analysing their generated/simulated data. Our platform provides several features but mainly:

1. *Data Diversity and Semantics:* OpenCEMS considers a variety of data sources (i.e., from sensors, documents, external sources, APIs, and simulators). In addition, the platform handles different datatypes (e.g., structured, unstructured, semi-structured). To consider data semantics, OpenCEMS allows the integration of domain-specific knowledge and components. This allows consider specificities related to equipment, data, and vocabularies according to the application domain (e.g., medical, commercial, agriculture).
2. *Environment Modeling and Monitoring:* OpenCEMS considers various connected environment components (e.g., devices, sensors, infrastructures, services) and defines the interactions between them. This entails providing users with means of customizing the graphical representation of all components. OpenCEMS is also domain specific in the representation of the connected environment (i.,e., front-end and back-end interfaces) by allowing users/administrators to generate personalized forms/interfaces for domain-specific components.
3. *Data Management Services:* OpenCEMS provides a plethora of services that consider connected environment requirements for pre-processing (e.g., management of mismatching formats, redundancies, anomalies, obsolescence), processing (e.g., exploratory data analysis, predictions, event detection) and post-processing (e.g., data/result visualisation). For instance, OpenCEMS provides automatic detection and correction of missing, anomalous and erroneous data. Indeed, data generated from connected devices may include several errors and anomalies due to the sensor failure or to data transfer issues, which badly impact the precision of the processes that ingest data to generate information, knowledge, and decision making insights.
4. *User-friendly:* Connected environment occupants/users might be unfamiliar with the technicalities required when handing connected environments and data analysis tools. Therefore, OpenCEMS provides easy to use graphical interfaces for environment creation and management (e.g., dropping pins on a smart city map, visual 2D/3D editor for building modeling, configuring components through web forms). Moreover, the platform provides pre-configured data management and analysis services as well as guidance for the user when he/she decides to configure a specific service. Finally, the platform provides a user-friendly graphical dashboard for service composition.
5. *Technical Flexibility:* OpenCEMS runs on an underlying micro-service architecture that provides extensibility (i.e., easy addition of new components/services), interoperability (i.e., means for adequate coupling of modules/services), and flexibility of data storage solutions. In addition, the platform allows the integration of external modules/developments. Thanks to its

architecture, the platform's services can be executed individually, or composed together manually or automatically. Moreover, our platform architecture allows it to easily evolve with emerging/future needs. This is important since by nature connected environments are a cyber representation of the real world that often evolves.

The remainder of this paper is organised as follows. Section 2 provides a deep review of the existing academic and commercial data analytics tools. A summary of the reviewed tools is then presented. In Sect. 3, we thoroughly describe the architecture and the different components of our proposal OpenCEMS. A use case scenario of OpenCEMS is then presented in Sect. 4. The last section concludes this paper and pins down future improvements of OpenCEMS.

2   Related Works

In the literature, several academic and industrial data analytics tools have been proposed. In order to compare them, we propose several criteria summarized in Table 1.

In the following, we review existing approaches and tools before comparing them. It is worthy to note that as surveyed in [14,16], most of existing platforms are domain oriented like transportation [6,7,41], healthcare [1,8,15,18,36,37], smart data management [5,38], and smart cities [9,11,13,17,19,30,31]. Industrial solutions can be Network-oriented or Data-oriented. Network-oriented solutions (e.g., Senso Go[5], Datadog IoT Monitoring[6], Senseye PdM[7], SkySpark[8], TeamViewer IoT[9], Domotz[10], AWS IoT Device Management[11]) provide platforms to manage IoT devices and diverse functionalities such as data analytics, predictive maintenance, monitoring and security.

In the following, we limit our review to generic data-oriented CE frameworks only. Network-oriented solutions won't be further detailed as well since they are mainly limited to device/equipment management and monitoring.

2.1   Research/Academic Works

Since recently, Data Analytics and specially Big Data Analytics (BDA) for connected environments has been an attractive research topic [2,14,16,26,32,35]. An architecture for Cognitive Internet of Things (CIoT) and big data has been proposed in [33]. CIoT integrates the Data Lake and Data Warehouse to collect heterogeneous data. It is based on a traditional process of data flow which

---

[5] https://sensu.io/iot-monitoring-with-sensu.

[6] https://www.datadoghq.com/dg/monitor/iot/.

[7] https://www.senseye.io/.

[8] https://skyfoundry.com/.

[9] https://www.teamviewer.com/en-us/iot/.

[10] https://www.domotz.com/.

[11] https://aws.amazon.com/iot-device-management/.

Table 1. List of comparative criteria

Criterion	Description	Possible Values
Environment Modeling (C1)	This criterion denotes the platform's ability to represent the connected environment components.	• Infrastructure • Sensor Network
Data Science Services (C2)	This criterion indicates the data science services covered by a platform.	• Data Cleaning & Refinement • Advanced ML-based processing • Post-processing
Data Source Diversity (C3)	This criterion denotes the platform's ability to consider a variety of data sources as input for the proposed services.	• Sensor Networks • Document Corpora • External Sources • Simulator
Datatype Diversity (C4)	This criterion denotes the platform's ability to handle different datatypes as input for the proposed services.	• Structured • Semi-structured • Unstructured
Service Deployment & Execution Modality (C5)	This criterion denotes the platform's ability to allow users various modalities for service deployment.	• Stand-alone • Service Composition
Required User Expertise (C6)	This criterion indicates the level of required user expertise when selecting, configuring, and executing data management services on a specific platform while considering the level of help/guidance that the platform offers to users.	• Low • Moderate • High
Ease Of Integration (C7)	This criterion denotes the platform's ability to be easily integrated with external complementary software/hardware components.	• Low • Moderate • High
Technical Flexibility (C8)	This criterion denotes the platform's technical flexibility in terms of easily extending existing functionality (e.g., adding new modules, services, and components), interconnecting different modules (e.g., aligning ontologies, connecting services for chain execution), and having flexible data storage solutions (i.e., changing the storage solution/strategy without modifying the underlying infrastructure).	• Extensible • Interoperable • Flexible
Domain-centric Processing (C9)	This criterion indicates if the platform provides contextual data management services related to specific real-world/simulated environments	• Yes • No

includes data source, collection, Extract Transform Load (ETL), business analytics and service.

In [10], authors proposed an Analytics Everywhere framework which performs: i) storage, computation, processing on distributed computational nodes such as cloud, fog, edge nodes; ii) descriptive, diagnostic, and predictive analytics; and iii) data life cycle management (e.g., data aggregation, contextualisation, transformation, and extraction). The framework has been applied on a real-world scenario for the management of a public transit. Authors in [27] described their vision of a platform for real-time data pre-processing and analytics using FOG-engines. The proposed architecture considers a set of data sources obtained from sensors, IoT devices, Web, and Corpora. It performs data pre-processing (cleaning, filtering, integration, ETL), storage, data mining, and analytics.

The work in [39] proposed a platform which combines IoT and Big Data Analytics (BDA) technology with fog and cloud computing. The system performs processing of a huge smart home IoT data in distributed fog nodes. The platform supports different operations: integration, processing, and analytics of smart home data. In order to evaluate the system, the authors analyze the smart home IoT data for predictive analytics of energy consumption behaviour.

In [12], an architecture for processing heterogeneous data in the Internet of Things was proposed. It includes three layers: i) *data sources* (e.g., smart water meters); ii) *data processing* which transforms and processes the data received from the sources; and iii) *data consumers* such as the end-user devices or services which use the processed information. In [34], the authors described a framework that integrates semantic data modelling, big data analytics, and learning models. The conceptual framework consists of five layers: i) *data acquisition* which collects data from sources such as sensors; ii) *extract-transform-load (ETL)* which is based on sensor drivers for each sensor that parse and convert collected data via semantic technologies into RDF (Resource Description Framework) form; iii) *semantic-rule reasoning*; iv) *learning layer* which extracts features from the data and builds machine learning models; and v) *action layer* evaluates the results of the learning layer and provides necessary actions. However, this framework has not been implemented.

Recently, the work described in [14] proposed a domain-independent Big Data Analytics based IoT architecture which is composed of six layers: i) *Data Manager* which collects raw data generated from the physical IoT objects sources; ii) *System Resources Controller* which process data by using data mining techniques; iii) *System Recovery Manager* which deploys predictive analytics over the data collected; iv) *BDA Handler* which performs data analytics (i.e. Data Aggregation, reduction; analysis, interpretation, visualization); (v) *Software Engineering Handler* which covers the main concepts of software engineering in order to ensure the overall system QoS (e.g. scalability, reusability, maintainability); and vi) *Security Manager* which aims to assure system security. As claimed by the authors, the proposed architecture stands for a potential solution for online-based data analysis in IoT-based systems but no technical and/or implementation issues has been provided.

Several real-time processing solutions are proposed. In [21], a platform for processing real-time (streaming) data from sensors has been developed and tested in a healthcare scenario. The platform is composed of three layers: i) *Data acquisition*; ii) *Data processing*; and iii) *Data storage and visualization*. The work in [28] presented SenSquare which is a collaborative IoT platform able to manage heterogeneous data coming from different sources (e.g., open IoT platforms and crowdsensing campaigns). SenSquare allows users to aggregate raw data streams and compose their own services through either a web interface or a mobile application, that can be exploited by other users. SnappyData [29] is an another open source platform for real time operational analytics. SnappyData integrates continuous stream processing, online transaction processing (OLTP), and online analytical processing (OLAP). In [40], Firework, a computing framework for big data processing and sharing in an IoT-based collaborative edge environment, is presented. Firework consists of three layers: i) *Service Management* which achieves service discovery and deployment; ii) *Job Management* which manages tasks running on a computing node; and iii) *Executor Management* that allocates computing resources to tasks. Firework provides programming user interfaces to interact with existing services and deploy Internet of Everything applications across geographically distributed computation resources. Evaluation performed on a real-time video analytics scenario shows that Firework reduces response latencies and network bandwidth cost.

Table 2 compares the different approaches presented here with respect to the aforementioned criteria.

Table 2. Academic frameworks comparison

	C1	C2	C3	C4	C5	C6	C7	C8	C9
[29]	Ø	{P,Post-p}	Ω	Struct	SCM	High	High	{Flex,Ext}	No
[27]	I	Ω	Ω	{Semi-Struct,Struct}	SCM	-	-	Ext	Yes
[10]	{I,SN}	Ω	SN	{Struct,unStruct}	SCM	-	-	{Flex,Ext}	Yes
[21]	SN	Ω	SN	Struct	SAM	High	-	Ext	Yes
[28]	{I,SN}	{Pre-P,Post-p}	{SN, ES}	Struct	SCM	High	-	Ext	Yes
[33]	SN	{Pre-P,P}	Ω	Ω	SCM	-	-	{Flex,Ext}	Yes
[39]	SN	Ω	Ω	Unstruct	SAM	-	Low	{Flex,Ext}	Yes
[12]	SN	Ω	SN	Ω	SCM	-	-	{Flex,Ext}	Yes
[40]	SN	{Pre-P,P}	{SN, Sim}	Unstruct	SCM	High	-	-	Yes
[34]	SN	{Pre-P,P,Post-p}	{SN, Sim}	Unstruct	SCM	High	-	-	No

Acronyms: Infrastructure (I), Sensor Network (SN), Pre-processing (Pre-p), Processing (P), Post-processing (Post-p), Document Corpora (DC), External Sources (ES), Simulated (Sim), Structured (Struct), Semi-Structured (Semi-Struct), Unstructured (Unstruct), Stand-Alone Mode (SAM), Service Composition Mode (SCM), Extensible (Ext), Interoperable (Int), Flexible (Flex), All (Ω), Not Applicable (-), None (Ø).

With regard to the environment modeling (C1), the reviewed frameworks are able to represent sensor networks and most of them manage structured data (C4). However, none of them is based on the use of external resources (like ontologies) to represent the connected environment. Concerning data mining services (C2), one can notice that most of these frameworks perform the three phases: i) pre-processing; ii) processing ; iii) post-processing but few of them integrate predictive analytics. Concerning the criteria (C6) and (C7), they are not covered in the majority of works.

2.2   Industrial Solutions

The commercial analytics industry has been through a sea of change in a short span of time and it is continuing to face rapid change and revolutionary development. Thus, the demand for industrial data management solutions is mature and filled with outstanding products for a range of applications, verticals, implementation strategies and budgets. In the following, we briefly describe the main tools provided by 'mega-vendors' such as Google, IBM, Microsoft, and Amazon.

- **BigQuery** (See footnote 1): is a Data Analytics tool proposed by Google and based on a RESTful web service that enables massive interactive analysis of large data sets in conjunction with Google repository. Google BigQuery is a Service (SaaS) that can be used in addition to MapReduce. It is a serverless mode and there is no infrastructure to manage. This tool allows to analyze data, organize, deploy, and test prediction models that are located in a logical Google warehouse. However, this tool, is free up to 1 TB of analyzed data per month and 10 GB of stored data. The main limitation of this tool, is its dependency to other google products (such as firebase, Google APIs and necessity of a Google account). Added to that, the BigQuery tool is unable to model a connected environment (criterion C1). Furthermore, it does not have any data imputation and correction solutions.
- **Watson Studio** (See footnote 2): is a powerful Data Analytics tools proposed by IBM. It is a flexible cloud-based solution allowing the automation of all the stages of data science projects. It provides interesting features allowing to import datasets from different sources, organize datasets in catalogs shared between authorized users, automatically detect missing or anomalous data, create visualizations and interactive dashboards, automatically create, optimize, deploy, and evaluate predictive models. However, IBM Watson Studio does not support connected environment modeling. In addition, it does not provide advanced solutions for data imputation and correction.
- **Amazon AWS** (See footnote 3): is a very efficient service that supplies cloud computing platforms (PaaS) for the customers who can be: an individual, a company or a government. Amazon Web Services (AWS) allows the customers to model, deploy, store, analyse, build real and virtual physical objects or even applications such as services. Moreover, it delivers a large amount of services that facilitate the usage for users that don't have much knowledge in the technology domain. However, despite all these benefits, AWS doesn't cover our C1 criterion (i.e., doesn't allow to model connected environments). Besides, it is not an open solution and is more expensive than other existing ones.
- **Azure Analysis Services** (See footnote 4): is the data analysis tool offered by Microsoft Azure. Based on the Microsoft SQL Server Analysis Services, it works as a service (PaaS). This tool provides enterprise-class BI semantic modeling capabilities and allows to benefit from the advantages of the cloud in terms of scalability, flexibility and management. However, Azure Analysis Services does not support connected environment modeling (criterion C1).

Also, it does not provide advanced solutions for data imputation and correction.

Table 3. Related works comparison

	C1	C2	C3	C4	C5	C6	C7	C8	C9
Google	{I,SN}	Ω	Ω	Ω	SAM	High	Moderate	Flex	Yes
IBM	{AD}	Ω	{ES,DC}	Ω	SAM	High	High	Ext	Yes
Amazon AWS	{I,SN}	Ω	Ω	Ω	SCM	Low	Moderate	Flex	Yes
Microsoft Azure	{I,SN}	Ω	{SN,ES}	Ω	SAM	High	High	Ext	Yes

Acronyms: Infrastructure (I), Sensor Network (SN), Pre-processing (Pre-p), Processing (P), Post-processing (Post-p), Document Corpora (DC), External Sources (ES), Simulated (Sim), Structured (Struct), Semi-Structured (Semi-Struct), Unstructured (Unstruct), Stand-Alone Mode (SAM), Service Composition Mode (SCM), Extensible (Ext), Interoperable (Int), Flexible (Flex), All (Ω), Not Applicable (-), None ($\emptyset$).

Table 3 summarises a comparison between the existing industrial analytics tools based on the aforementioned criteria. Indeed, the major common limitation of those tools is related to the first criterion C1 (environment modeling) since all of them are unable to represent the connected environment components and specificities. Moreover, IBM and Microsoft azure are unable to consider a variety of data sources as input like Document Corpora and simulated data for there proposed services. To sum-up, most of those industrial solutions are expensive and highly dependent on there own technologies.

3 Proposal: OpenCEMS

In this section, we present the OpenCEMS platform and its key components. We will start by emphasizing on data modeling, querying, user profiles, and the technical infrastructure. Thereafter, we detail two main aspects: data management services and automatic web forms generation (i.e., easy to use and adapted graphical interfaces for non expert users).

As illustrated in Fig. 1, OpenCEMS allows users to easily create, manage, and maintain one or several connected environments. In each CE, it is possible to add and configure infrastructures (e.g., cities, buildings, homes, grids) while specifying spatial settings on a graphical map using a 2D/3D modeling tool (cf. Criterion C1). Moreover, from the front-end user interfaces, the users can deploy various devices/data sources in their environments. They can integrate: real devices, simulated devices, external sources, mobile phones, and files (cf. Criterion C3).

These sources generate a huge amount of data that is collected and sent to the platform for storage. Furthermore, the data can be managed using a plethora of provided web services (e.g., anomaly detection, data formatting, redundancy management, clustering, prediction, and data visualization) (cf. Criterion C2). The user is able to track and export both devices' data and services results' data through the platform.

Interestingly enough, OpenCEMS aims to free users from technical limitations and restrictions that might make the management of complex connected

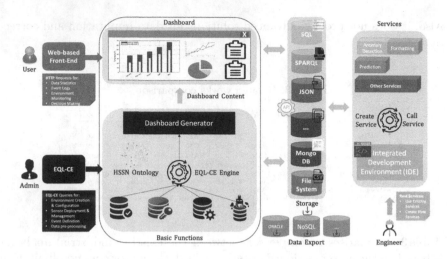

Fig. 1. OpenCEMS framework

environments time-consuming and difficult. Therefore, to ensure that the platform is flexible, extensible, and easy to use, the back-end assists and supports users in the following aspects:

– **Environment Modeling:** OpenCEMS relies on the HSSN ontology [23] where infrastructures, platforms, devices/sensors, and data are represented. HSSN defines the structure and specifics of each component/entity that the user deploys/generates on the platform (e.g., buildings, devices, sensor observations). Moreover, in order to allow personalized and domain oriented connected environment components, administrators can align it to an application domain ontology and customize the web forms that describe any entity based on the ontology concepts (cf. Criterion C1).
– **Querying and Event Detection:** Users can interact with the platform using the front-end graphical interface (clicking, dropping pins on the map), or by submitting queries (e.g., create a component, insert a instance of a sensor, update the structure of a building, delete already deployed devices) via the console terminal. For the latter, the platform provides EQL-CE [24], an event query language specifically designed for connected environments. The language can be used by administrators to easily assist front-end users by maintaining, altering, or evolving their respective connected environments (cf. Criteria C6, C9).
– **Storage Flexibility:** To avoid data serialization and storage issues, OpenCEMS provides an array of data storage solutions (e.g., RDF triple store for semantic data, document-based storage repositories for document corpora). The technicalities of different storage systems and how they affect querying and data processing are kept transparent to the user so that he/she doesn't have to deal with complex data-base realted operations. In addition, one could export the data locally for private storage (cf. Criterion C8).

– **Service Support:** Raw data originating from integrated devices/data sources suffers from various inconsistencies (e.g., anomalies, missing values, duplicates). Therefore, OpenCEMS provides users with inter-operable web services for pre-processing (e.g., management of mismatching formats, redundancies, anomalies, obsolescence, missing data), processing (e.g., exploratory data analysis, predictions, event detection) and post-processing (e.g., data/result visualisation). These services could be executed in a stand-alone mode, or in orchestrated compositions using a graphical service composer [20]. Finally, to ensure extensibility, the platform provides an Integrated Development Environment (IDE) where specific users (i.e., engineers or developers) can add, modify, and delete services (cf. Criteria C2, C5).

3.1 Technical Overview

As depicted in Fig. 2, the technical architecture of OpenCEMS platform is composed of the following four layers:

1. **Client Layer:** refers to client interfaces for the development, modeling, analysis, presentation, reporting, and delivery of various content.
2. **API Gateway:** is an abstraction layer for accessing a service. It manages the user request by invoking a number of micro-services and returning the results. Indeed, it could be seen as a single point of entry for external users to access a given service.
3. **Containers' Orchestrations:** is composed of several types of micro-services. The first one includes python scripts that implement traditional machine learning algorithms using the classic library Anaconda[12] that contains different tools like: Pandas, NumPy, PyTorch, Scikit-Learn, and Keras. The second one contains the spark streaming processing tool. It is a single engine supporting both batch and streaming workflows natively. Spark Streaming[13] allows live streaming data analysis for scalable, high-throughput, and fault-tolerant stream processing. The third type is composed of Node JS scripts that call a SPARQL client in order to interface Apache Jena Fuseki[14] for ontology management and storage. Besides, each deployed micro-service is containerized in a Docker container. We used an orchestrator (Kubernetes) allowing the transparent management of the containers. In particular, it automates the container execution, and adds scalability to the system by offering container load balancing (cf. Criteria C7, C8).
4. **Data Storage:** is achieved through: i) NoSQL for the big data and the real time storage; ii) Json format for storing the simulation logs; and iii) the event query language EQL [22] for the CE modeling and simulation (cf. Criterion C4).

---

[12] https://www.anaconda.com.
[13] https://spark.apache.org.
[14] https://jena.apache.org.

In the following, we first detail the main existing data management services provided by the OpenCEMS platform. Then, we present the ontology-based web form generation services of the connected environment.

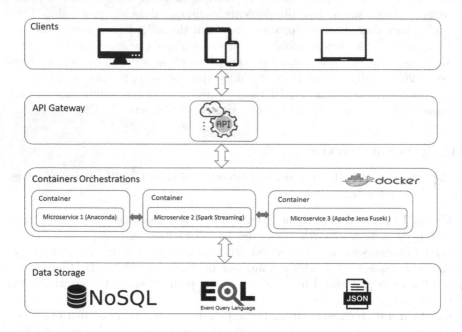

Fig. 2. OpenCEMS technical architecture

3.2 Data Management Services

OpenCEMS offers the users diverse services allowing them to explore and analyze data (cf. Criterion C2). Each service is deployed separately in a Docker container and has a REST API enabling inter and intra-applications interaction (cf. Criterion C7). The proposed services can be classified into five main categories: data generation/storage, data retrieval, data pre-processing, advanced data processing, data post-processing services. In the following, we briefly introduce each category:

3.2.1 Data Acquisition, Storage and Retrieval. As stated before, OpenCEMS provides users with numerous ways to gather, generate, or retrieve data (cf. Criterion C3). Many collection methods are proposed according to the deployed device/data source:

– **Real devices:** OpenCEMS allows to integrate and connect any devices composed of sensors and a microprocessor (e.g., raspberry, Arduino). They can

Fig. 3. Simulated devices form

be directly installed at the customer's site in order to capture the real phenomena of their physical environment. The users must first choose the desired environmental parameters. Then, a device containing all the suitable sensors will be provided. Indeed, the latter measures the requested data and sends them to the platform for storage.

– **Simulated devices:** OpenCEMS allows to simulate virtual devices that can be created on-demand. To do that, users can provide the related parameters to simulate the corresponding behaviour and define data generation and timing constraints. Figure 3 shows the creation form of a device. The first toggle consists of providing basic information about the device while specifying its type (e.g., static, mobile). The second one allows the creation of sensors to be associated with the device, And finally the last toggle allows the association of documents to the device.

– **External sources:** OpenCEMS supplies users with many protocols (e.g., HTTP, MQTT, AMQP) and connectors to external APIs (e.g., Weather API, Words API). Users must initially select a supportable protocol for their external sources. Then, they need to describe the data they are delivering. Regardless of the selected protocol, they will receive the proper configuration settings

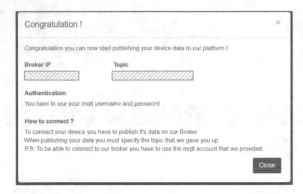

Fig. 4. Mqtt configuration settings

allowing them to successfully publish data from their devices. For example, as shown in Fig. 4, when selecting the MQTT protocol, users get a broker URI along with many required topics. Whereas, when choosing HTTP, they obtain a resource URI, as well as the required method and parameters.

– **Mobile phones:** OpenCEMS provides a mobile application that measures and senses the mobile crowd-sourced data (e.g., accelerometer, gyroscope, ambient light, ambient noise, proximity, GPS, camera) before pushing it into the platform. Users need to install the application on their mobile phones. Then, they have to enable (or disable) the desired (or unwanted) mobile crowd-sourced data. By doing so, the mobile application will gather and send the wanted parameters to the platform.

– **Files:** OpenCEMS allows also users to import files as external data sources using their dashboard.

Several NoSQL data storage systems are available in OpenCEMS. More precisely, they can be classified into two categories: graph databases and document databases. The graph database is used for knowledge graph storage (i.e., ontology storage, RDF triple stores). It stores the definition and some data of connected environments, devices, sensors, and services. Whereas the document-based database is used to store users' files and document corpora. In particular, Jena fuseki is used as a graph-based storage system, while MongoDB is used as a document-based storage system. (cf. Criterion C4) It is important to note that storing data in the ontology has a lot of benefits, especially in connected environments. It leads to the inference and enrichment of new knowledge from initial information. As an example, storing services definition in the ontology will help inferring various service compositions. Several services were developed in order to store data in these two databases. They first establish a connection with the proper storage to save afterward the data in the designated system.

Figure 5 depicts the process of calling the storage services. Effectively, a messaging broker is deployed. The device acts as a publisher, while a developed controller acts as a subscriber. After data gathering, the device will publish, to

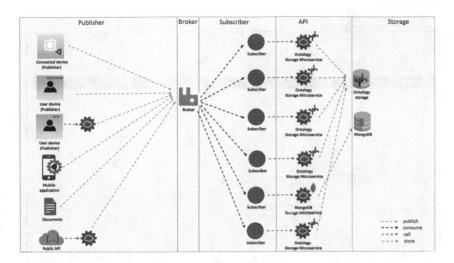

Fig. 5. Data collection framework

the broker, a message that encapsulates the data in a JSON string format. Each device, depending on its type and characteristics, sends subjects along with the message. Thereafter, thanks to the topics, a suitable controller will receive the message, parse it, and then call an adequate storage.

All data and files originating from the connected devices can be fetched, edited, or deleted through many developed services. In fact, each data, depending on its type and its purpose, has an appropriate service allowing the user to retrieve, update or remove it from its dedicated storage system. Here are two examples of data retrieval services implemented in OpenCEMS:

– A service that connects to the document database (e.g., MongoDB) in order to read and manage user documents. It is used to render the documents of a specific user.
– Another service that interfaces the graph database (e.g., Jena Fuseki) to fetch and control the service definitions. For example, it can be used by service composer to retrieve compatible services.

3.2.2 Data Pre-processing. Data pre-processing is essential before performing any analysis or launching Machine Learning processes. It detects inconsistent, abnormal, missing, redundant, noisy, obsolete, or unnecessary data then provides suitable solutions to address the aforementioned issues in order to improve data quality and availability. In what follows, we details main services:

– **Missing Data Management:** This service detects missing data and replaces them with other values. It works with various types of datasets. Specifically, it handles time-series data. In fact, it can deal with regular, irregular, multivariate, or monovariate datasets. It is divided into several phases. In the former,

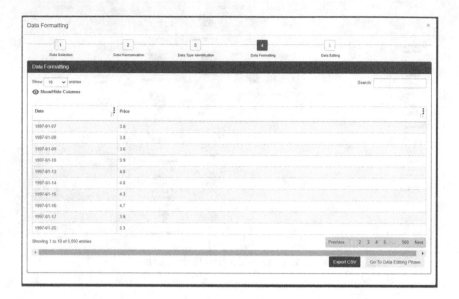

Fig. 6. Data formatting

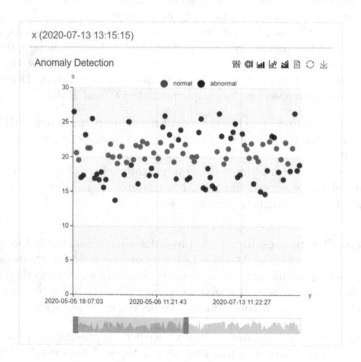

Fig. 7. Anomaly detection

datetime	temperature	echauffement	heure	hm	month	weekday	
2018-11-18 09:30:00	283.8166667	false	9	950	11	6	
2018-11-18 09:40:00	283.9277778	false	9	966	11	6	
2018-11-18 09:50:00	284.0388889	false	9	983	11	6	
2018-11-18 10:00:00	284.15	false	10	1000	11	6	
2018-11-18 10:10:00	284.3611111	false	10	1016	11	6	
2018-11-18 10:20:00	284.5722222	false	10	1033	11	6	
2018-11-18 10:30:00	284.7833333000001	false	10	1050	11	6	
2018-11-18 10:40:00	284.9944444	false	10	1066	11	6	
2018-11-18 10:50:00	285.2055556	false	10	1083	11	6	

Fig. 8. Prediction

Fig. 9. Model representation

the dataset is checked for regularity. If irregular time steps are detected, it uses a set of resampling tools to convert the subset of data into a regular one. In the next phase, it checks if one or more variables are detected within the data (mono/multivariate data). Indeed, handling missing data might require different techniques for each detected variables depending on data statistics

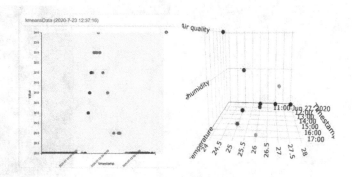

Fig. 10. Hard clustering

Fig. 11. Clustering hierarchical

and the value distribution of each of the aforementioned variables. Therefore, it handles multivariate time-series separately by splitting a multivariate data sets into multiple mono-variate data sets. In the last phase, missing data management solutions are applied. Indeed, there are several efficient solutions to deal with missing data. Those solutions are either statistical (e.g., mean imputation methods, previous imputation methods, interpolation) or machine learning based methods (e.g., Incremental Space-Time-based model (ISTM) methods). An adequate solution will be executed based on user's choice. As results, the service returns the score, the consumed processing time, and the cleaned dataset.

- **Data Redundancy Management:** Connected environments typically generate huge amounts of redundant data. This is often the result of various factors (e.g., dense deployment of sensors in specific areas, continuous sensing during uneventful periods of time). Therefore, the system ends up storing a significant amount of unnecessary data that consumes storage space, slows down data retrieval, and makes processing with resource consuming tools more complex. To address this issue, we propose a set of services for data redundancy management that analyze the data, clusters redundant/duplicate data objects, and proposes various ways of either removing or summarizing the redundancies. More details about these services can be found in [25].

- **Data Formatting:** In OpenCEMS platform, data can be originated from many heterogeneous sensors or data sources. This emphasizes how crucial data format validation is. That's why, we propose various formatting functionalities (auto-detection of delimiters, file conversions, datasets merging, classical editing, etc.) but mainly harmonizing the data in each variable related to the same feature (e.g., temperature, CO2) into a unique format. For example, a data subset containing several timestamp formats (e.g., ISO, UNIX), will be converted to one with a single format selected by the user (e.g., ISO format). Similarly, if it holds different decimal formats (e.g., US, Europe), it will be transformed into a unique one. We also allow to format data of the selected variable: Transform a string to a capital case, lower case, camel case, and so on. One can also format decimals by choosing the number of digits after the decimal point. For example, in Fig. 6, the variable price was formatted with one decimal digit.

- **Data Standardization and Normalization:** In many cases, it is not possible to immediately apply a processing operation (such as prediction, or anomaly detection) on a dataset. It becomes then necessary to normalize or modify the data. For example, numerous machine learning algorithms work only with numeric values. Thus, it is required to convert the string values into numeric one. Another example includes algorithms that only treat data between 0 and 1. If the available data set includes data from another range, it is essential to standardize it. To fulfill the previously described needs, the data standardization and normalization service is implemented. Indeed, it proposes several normalization and scaling techniques (e.g., pre-process scaler, label encoder, standard scaler).

– **Anomaly Detection Services:** It is used to identify abnormal values sensed
  by a set of sensors. Many classification methods are used to achieve this
  goal (e.g., k-Nearest Neighbors, Support Vector Machine, Bayesian, Decision
  Tree). To use this service, one must first select which variable should be
  checked for anomalies (such as temperature, humidity), before selecting the
  appropriate pre-built model. In case the user wants to build a new model, she
  has to specify the training dataset, the necessary method, and the dependent
  and independent variables. As a result, the service supplies a labeled dataset
  describing anomalies. In addition, as shown in Fig. 7, the user has the possibility to visualize results in a graphical user-friendly format, where anomalies
  are highlighted using several styling patterns (e.g., colors, line styles, font
  weight).

3.2.3 Advanced Data Processing. The services proposed in this category
are used to perform analysis and launch machine learning processes in order to
gain more insights and knowledge. More precisely:

– **Exploratory Data Analysis:** OpenCEMS provides various methods for
  exploring data sources and extracting several interesting metrics and characteristics. As examples, here are some methods supplied by this category:
    • Supply data statistics of the chosen variable related to the same feature
      (e.g., count, maximum, mean, minimum, and standard deviation values).
    • Retrieve all types existing in a data subset as well as their percentages
      (e.g., decimal 50%, Boolean 20%, string 30%).
    • Generate file meta-data/statistics to the users (e.g., file size, number of
      variables, number of rows).
– **Prediction Service:** OpenCEMS allows users to predict a phenomenon
  within the CE using supervised learning techniques. It consists of evaluating
  the relative impact of a predictor (i.e., independent variable(s)) on a particular outcome (i.e., dependent variable). Several regressions (e.g., Multiple Linear Regression, Support Vector Regression), neural networks, and time-series
  forecasting (e.g., Long Short-Term memory, Bidirectional Long Short-Term
  Memory, Gated Recurrent Unit) methods are implemented. They basically
  include two phases: Training and Prediction. In the training phase, the user
  must first select the dataset, the methods, the independent variables, and
  the dependent variable. Then, the needed method will be called thereafter to
  build the model. At the end of the model creation, the user will receive it as
  output as well as several evaluation scores. In the prediction phase, the user
  can choose the dataset to predict and the adequate model to use. As a result,
  a predicted file will be returned to the user. Figure 8 illustrates the prediction
  output as a table with the predicted value highlighted in yellow. It is worth
  mentioning that the users are able to visualize in a very intuitive way all built
  models with all their information (e.g., applied method, the parameters and
  the dataset used along with the evaluation scores gotten). Figure 9 shows the
  model representation. Moreover, OpenCEMS tries to assist users to choose
  the best model, by offering them an appropriate interface to compare models.

- **Clustering Service:** It is one of the data mining services implemented in OpenCEMS. Unlike the classification service, this one does not require a training phase. It is essentially used to group similar devices, sensors, or data into the same cluster. For this purpose, various clustering methods are offered to the users. They can be categorized into two main branches: Hard Clustering and Soft Clustering. In fact, each element in hard clustering must belong to only one cluster, whereas in soft clustering, it might belong to multiple clusters. Density-based, Spectral clustering, k-means, k-medoids, and Mean-shift create hard clusters while hierarchical algorithms build soft ones. To execute this service, the users are requested to choose one of the existing methods with all its required parameters. As an output, they receive a JSON message describing the resulted clusters. Moreover, users benefit from a variety of graphics that illustrate better those clusters and their elements (e.g., 2D graphs, 3D graphs, dendograms, and pie charts). Figure 10 displays the result of a hard clustering while Fig. 11 shows the result of a hierarchical clustering.
- **Topic Extraction Service:** It is an NLP based service utilized for document mining. Indeed, it mainly aims to extract and organize textual documents into a set of topics (where a topic represents a word or a sentence that clearly defines the entire documents). This service is developed using an unsupervised technique: Latent Dirichlet Allocation or LDA. It implements various functionalities: topic generation, topics word matrix construction which contains topics with their corresponding probabilities, and coherence calculation. Besides, this service can work in three modes:
  - Topic extraction: In this mode, the user must choose some required parameters in order to run the LDA algorithm.
  - Automated topic extraction: In this mode, the LDA algorithm is improved. Unlike the first, it does not require user intervention to run the algorithm. This means the user is not required to select parameters in order to execute the algorithm. Automatic parameters tuning will take place. In other words, all possible parameters combinations will be tested, until they identify the best ones.
  - Topic discovery and hierarchy: In this mode, topics will be collected and extracted from a corpus. Subsequently, from these generated topics, other topics will be extracted (i.e., topics of topics). Throughout the entire process, an identification of the relations between document and topic, and topic and topic will take place.

3.2.4 Data Post-processing. Post-processing services allow users to visualise and understand their results. Indeed, simulated or real-world data are stored in a machine readable formats but they are not understandable by a human. For this purpose, OpenCEMS enables rich graphical representations (e.g., Map, 2D graphs, 3D graphs, tables, dendrograms) to help users explore correlations between variables, review outliers values. Two modes are provided:

- Embedded Data visualization is the use of our own computer-supported, visual representation of data. Unlike static data visualization, our interactive data visualization allows users to specify the format used in displaying

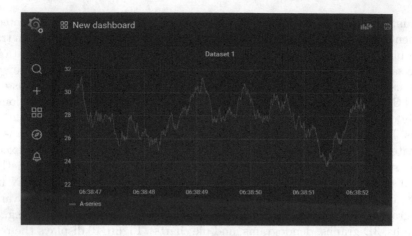

Fig. 12. Data visualization in grafana

data. Common visualization techniques are used such as: Line graphs, Bar charts, Scatter plots, and Pie charts.

– Grafana is one of the most popular dashboard and visualization tools for rendering data sources. It offers advanced data visualizing and querying features. Therefore, in order to benefit from its powerful functionalities, we have integrated it into our platform. In fact, data sources are loaded from our platform to grafana for visualization. Figure 12 shows a particular dataset visualized in grafana.

3.3 Services Execution Modalities

All the previously listed services are accessible from a web platform. Users can easily launch the service they need. In fact, OpenCEMS offers two modes for executing the needed services: standalone and service compositions modes. In the following, we briefly present each one.

3.3.1 Standalone Mode. For each service, there is an intuitively, and easy-to-use web form. Each one is composed of several buttons, labels, and inputs (e.g., text fields, select box, file input, and radio buttons) that represent the parameters of the deployed service (e.g., input dataset, algorithm parameters). In addition, users can specify how to visualize the results of the service (such as graphs, tables, and so on). At the end, once the users fill all the required form parameters, the service will be called, and thereafter a response will be displayed on their dashboard. It is important to note that the system provides users with assistance throughout the configuration steps. Furthermore, all service calls as well as their results are saved and displayed in the user's dashboard (cf. Criteria C5, C6).

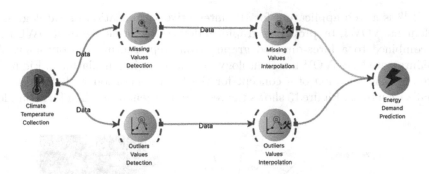

Fig. 13. Service composition at a glance

3.3.2   Service Composition Mode. It is beneficial to combine the afore-mentioned services to provide users with a highly powerful and flexible means. To do so, we relied on the services definitions stored in the ontology to enable the extraction and the inference of several semantic relations between services allowing compositions and recommendations. OpenCEMS proposes a user friendly composer to perform service compositions. To do so, the user drags and drops the desired services in the dedicated area, and then connects them together through the specific connectors. It's worth mentioning that the users are constantly provided with suggestions to know how to link services to each other (cf. Criteria C5, C6).

Furthermore, they are alerted when they attempt to link incompatibles services. Therefore, invalid and un-executable service compositions are prevented.

Figure 13 illustrates an example of service composition.

3.4   Ontology-Based Web Form Generation

Web input forms are a common tool to obtain data on the web. At present, many web forms still consist of plain-text input fields. While there are some options to declare the input types for a particular field, web forms are not able to obtain data in a semantically structured way that goes beyond primitive data types. In order to provide customized and domain oriented interfaces, we proposed Ontology-based Web Form Generation to define each form using the domain concepts. Thus, it utilises the connected environment as input and converts it into Visual Notation for OWL Ontology Language (VOWL) for the graphical representation of OWL elements. Once the elements are represented, the user could match each concept representing a component of the connected environment with the appropriate concept in a dedicated user interface ontology[15] that we introduce for this purpose.

Thereafter, a form builder is provided to generate the suitable form, for each connected environment component, using the user interface ontology. Web-

---

[15] https://opencems.fr/ontology/data/ui.owl.

VOWL[16] is a web application for the interactive visualization of ontologies. It implements VOWL by providing graphical depictions for elements of OWL that are combined to a force-directed graph layout representing the ontology. We have integrated WebVOWL for ontology visualization in our platform. Figure 14 represents the selection of a concept for the form generation with WebVOWL visualization tools. Figure 15 shows the result of the generation in a form builder.

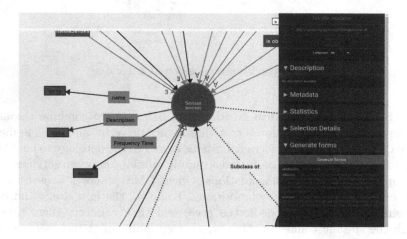

Fig. 14. Form ontology concept form

3.5   Ongoing Developments

There are numerous services being developed in addition to the previously described service set that OpenCEMS offers. In the following, we will give a quick introduction of a few of them.

– **Recommendation Modeling:** As discussed previously, many services, such as prediction and anomaly detection services, require a training phase to perform. In other words, they definitely need to build training models. Subsequently, there will be a large number of models created, making it difficult for the user to remember which model to apply to which dataset. For this reason, this service intends to assign an appropriate model to a dataset chosen by the user. In fact, similarity studies between the dataset labels and the model metadata will be carried to afterward select the best model. It is important to point out that an ontology is created in order to fully describe and detail each model, and thereafter facilitate the recommendation.
– **Data Obsolescence Management:** This service is intended to manage data obsolescence. In fact, in connected environments, data can become obsolete

---

[16] http://vowl.visualdataweb.org/webvowl.html.

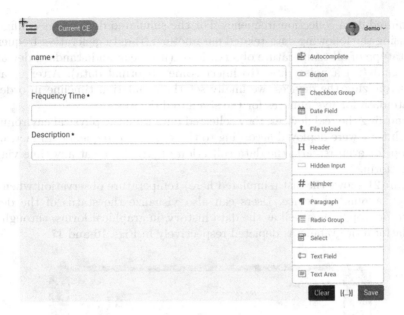

Fig. 15. On-the-fly generated form

due to numerous factors (e.g., the dynamism of the environment such as a change in sensor location, non-requesting of the data). This module is divided into two main categories. In the first one, data obsolescence is detected, while in the second, the latter is addressed (e.g., delete data, replace data with another storage).

4   Illustration Example

In this section, we want to give the reader an idea of how the OpenCEMS platform globally works. To do so, we consider the following scenario of a smart city where 5 static devices need to be deployed in a particular area to monitor temperature rises. The purpose of this illustration example is to show how the platform allows users to configure environments, devices/sensors, generate data, and then to utilize data management services.

4.1   Environment Setup and Data Acquisition

Once the user is logged in and selects to create a smart city environment, the map of the current user city is displayed (according to her location). The user only needs to click on each location desired to create devices. Figure 20 illustrates the aforementioned devices' cluster. In this example, we deployed the first two devices as real ones and the three remaining as simulated ones. We embedded one temperature sensor on each device. For the real devices, we defined the required data collection frequency. For the simulated devices, we configured them using the following data-related parameters: (i) data generation frequency; (ii) datatype of all temperature observations; (iii) mean and standard deviation values; and (iv) a noise ratio (to inject some abnormal data). After creating and customizing the devices, we finally set the simulation timeline in order to generate data for five minutes for the simulated devices.

Regarding the real devices, they collected data from the physical environment in which they were deployed according to the requested frequency. In fact, users can stop (or even restart) the data collection of any device at any time via the web platform.

Figure 21 shows the last (simulated here) temperature observation when one clicks on a plugged device. Users can also visualize the status of the device (started or stopped) as well as the data history, in graphical forms, through our web platform or grafana as depicted respectively in Figs. 16 and 17.

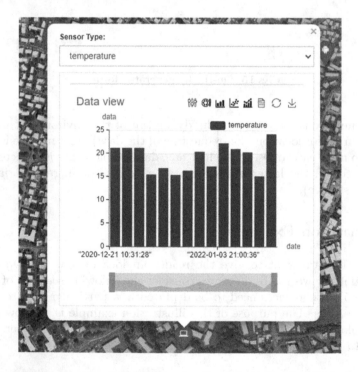

Fig. 16. Temperature data history visualized through the web platform

As explained earlier, it is possible to model and fine-tuned the environment by allowing users to design an interior space such as a house or an apartment and add devices and perform simulations. Thanks to our user-friendly interface, users can add doors, windows, add furnitures, draw walls and of course place devices in desired locations. Figure 18 shows the example of the creation of a building in 2D space while Fig. 19 shows an example of a 3D building space.

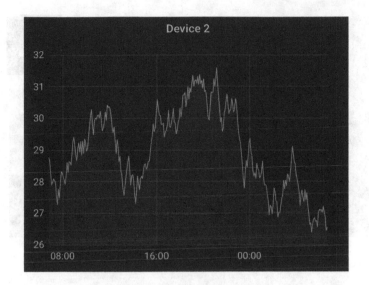

Fig. 17. Temperature data history visualized through grafana

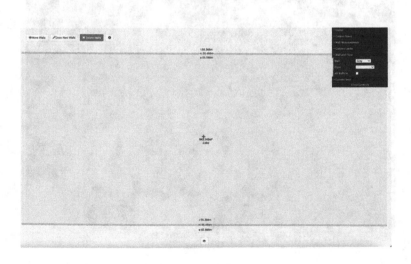

Fig. 18. 2D floorplan

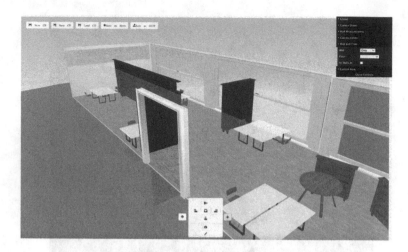

Fig. 19. Design in 3D

Fig. 20. Smart city

Fig. 21. Generated data

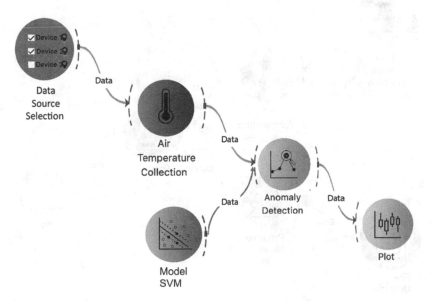

Fig. 22. Composition example of anomaly detection

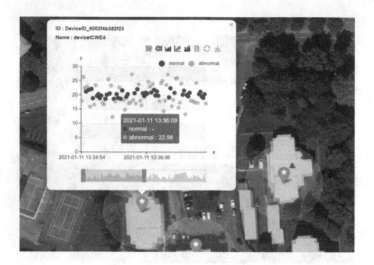

Fig. 23. Result visualisation

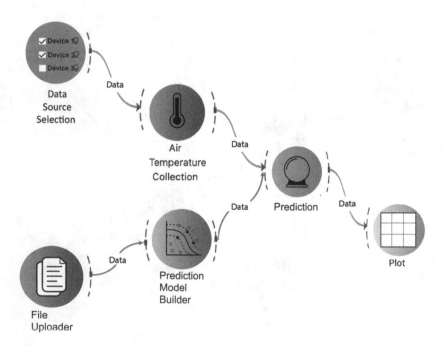

Fig. 24. Composition example of prediction

4.2   Services Usage

To illustrate the use of OpenCEMS services, we will present an example of anomaly detection and another one of phenomena prediction. More precisely, we will show how to run those two services. All other services can be operated and executed in the same manner. To demonstrate the execution process, we used here our graphical service composer. Obviously, we could have used the standalone mode in order to launch these services.

4.2.1   Anomaly Detection.

- **Service Composer:** We use the graphical service composer provided by the platform to create a composition that detects data anomalies from the observations generated during the previously discussed simulation. Figure 22 shows the anomaly detection composition. The generated temperature data is sent to the anomaly detection service. Using a pre-trained classification model (Support Vector Machine in this example) the anomaly detection service labels incoming sensor observations as normal or abnormal.
- **Data Visualisation:** The sensor observations and their corresponding labels (i.e., normal or abnormal) are sent to the data visualization service "Plot" where the user can view color coded sensor observations (e.g., blue for normal values and red for anomalies). The result is shown in Fig. 23. Indeed, users can customize the resulting graph. For example, they can: 1) rename the x-axis, y-axis, and the graph, 2) modify the color of the abnormal and normal data, 3) change the type of graph (i.e., scatter, bar chart), or 4) bound the graph between preferred timestamps. Furthermore, users can view and/or download the graph data as JSON output. They are also able to export the resulted graph as an image, or to grafana.

4.2.2   Phenomena Prediction.

- **Service Composer:** We construct the service composition represented in Fig. 24 in order to predict temperature by using sensors data. To do that, we first fetch the data of the needed devices before sending them to the prediction service. The latter requires a model to perform. That's why we build a training model by uploading a training dataset and sending it to the training service. Of course, users could select an existing pre-trained model instead of building a new one as we did in the anomaly detection example. As a result, the forecasting service outputs a file containing the predicted values.
- **Data Visualisation:** The prediction file is sent to the visualization service, which allows the users to visualize a table with the predicted attribute highlighted in yellow. The table is supplied with a toolbar allowing to customize it (i.e., change the color of the prediction attribute, change the name of the table, show/hide the columns). Moreover, it is possible to export it (as an image or into grafana).

5   Conclusion and Future Works

In this paper, we have introduced OpenCEMS, an open platform for data management and analytics in various application domains and contexts, and more specifically in designing CEs and analysing their generated/simulated data. By its easy use, OpenCEMS allows to graphically design and represent the different components of the CE and to define the interactions between them. Consequently, one can either: i) simulate data with respect to different setting parameters; or ii) contextualise real data collected from the connected devices. In addition, OpenCEMS provides a plethora of adapted and domain oriented services for automating the life cycle phases of data analytics projects. Each service is deployed separately following a micro-service oriented architecture, which enables other applications or micro-services to interact with it. We are constantly developing indexing services in order to locate and retrieve data in a faster and appropriate means.

References

1. Ahmadi, H., Arji, G., Shahmoradi, L., Safdari, R., Nilashi, M., Alizadeh, M.: The application of internet of things in healthcare: a systematic literature review and classification. Univ. Access Inf. Soc. **18**(4), 837–869 (2018). https://doi.org/10.1007/s10209-018-0618-4
2. Ahmed, E., et al.: The role of big data analytics in internet of things. Comput. Netw. **129**, 459–471 (2017)
3. Allani, S., Chbeir, R., Salameh, K.: Towards better data management/gathering in connected environments. In: Q2SWinet 2019 - Proceedings of the 15th ACM International Symposium on QoS and Security for Wireless and Mobile Networks, pp. 53–59 (2019)
4. Allani, S., Chbeir, R., Salameh, K., Yeferny, T.: Towards a Smarter Data dissemination strategy in connected environments. Procedia Comput. Sci. **176**, 1043–1052 (2020)
5. Arridha, R., Sukaridhoto, S., Pramadihanto, D., Funabiki, N.: Classification extension based on IoT-big data analytic for smart environment monitoring and analytic in real-time system. Int. J. Space Based Situated Comput. **7**(2), 82–93 (2017)
6. Asaithambi, S.P.R., Venkatraman, R., Venkatraman, S.: MOBDA: microservice-oriented big data architecture for smart city transport systems. Big Data Cogn. Comput. **4**(3), 17 (2020)
7. Balbin, P.P.F., Barker, J.C.R., Leung, C.K., Tran, M., Wall, R.P., Cuzzocrea, A.: Predictive analytics on open big data for supporting smart transportation services. In: Cristani, M., Toro, C., Zanni-Merk, C., Howlett, R.J., Jain, L.C. (eds.) Knowledge-Based and Intelligent Information & Engineering Systems: Proceedings of the 24th International Conference KES-2020, Virtual Event, 16–18 September 2020. Procedia Computer Science, vol. 176, pp. 3009–3018. Elsevier (2020)
8. Batko, K.M., Slezak, A.: The use of big data analytics in healthcare. J. Big Data **9**(1), 3 (2022)
9. Cano, M.V.M., et al.: Applicability of big data techniques to smart cities deployments. IEEE Trans. Ind. Inform. **13**(2), 800–809 (2017)

10. Cao, H., Wachowicz, M., Renso, C., Carlini, E.: Analytics everywhere: generating insights from the internet of things. IEEE Access **7**, 71749–71769 (2019)
11. Cavicchioli, R., Martoglia, R., Verucchi, M.: A novel real-time edge-cloud big data management and analytics framework for smart cities. J. Univers. Comput. Sci. **28**(1), 3–26 (2022)
12. Corral-Plaza, D., Medina-Bulo, I., Ortiz, G., Boubeta-Puig, J.: A stream processing architecture for heterogeneous data sources in the internet of things. Comput. Stand. Interfaces **70**, 103426 (2020)
13. Daissaoui, A., Boulmakoul, A., Karim, L., Lbath, A.: IoT and big data analytics for smart buildings: a survey. J. Ubiquitous Syst. Pervasive Networks **13**(1), 27–34 (2020)
14. Fawzy, D., Moussa, S.M., Badr, N.L.: The internet of things and architectures of big data analytics: challenges of intersection at different domains. IEEE Access **10**, 4969–4992 (2022)
15. Galetsi, P., Katsaliaki, K.: A review of the literature on big data analytics in healthcare. J. Oper. Res. Soc. **71**(10), 1511–1529 (2020)
16. Ge, M., Bangui, H., Buhnova, B.: Big data for internet of things: a survey. Future Gener. Comput. Syst. **87**, 601–614 (2018)
17. Gomes, E., Dantas, M.A.R., de Macedo, D.D.J., Rolt, C.R.D., Brocardo, M.L., Foschini, L.: Towards an infrastructure to support big data for a smart city project. In: Reddy, S., Gaaloul, W. (eds.) 25th IEEE International Conference on Enabling Technologies: Infrastructure for Collaborative Enterprises, WETICE 2016, Paris, France, 13–15 June 2016, pp. 107–112. IEEE Computer Society (2016)
18. Islam, M.S., Liu, D., Wang, K., Zhou, P., Yu, L., Wu, D.: A case study of healthcare platform using big data analytics and machine learning. In: Proceedings of the 2019 3rd High Performance Computing and Cluster Technologies Conference, pp. 139–146 (2019)
19. Jindal, A., Kumar, N., Singh, M.: A unified framework for big data acquisition, storage, and analytics for demand response management in smart cities. Future Gener. Comput. Syst. **108**, 921–934 (2020)
20. Kallab, L., Chbeir, R., Mrissa, M.: Automatic k-resources discovery for hybrid web connected environments. In: Bertino, E., Chang, C.K., Chen, P., Damiani, E., Goul, M., Oyama, K. (eds.) 2019 IEEE International Conference on Web Services, ICWS 2019, Milan, Italy, 8–13 July 2019, pp. 146–153. IEEE (2019). https://doi.org/10.1109/ICWS.2019.00034
21. Malek, Y.N., et al.: On the use of IoT and big data technologies for real-time monitoring and data processing. In: Shakshuki, E.M. (ed.) The 8th International Conference on Emerging Ubiquitous Systems and Pervasive Networks (EUSPN 2017) 18–20 September 2017, Lund, Sweden. Procedia Computer Science, vol. 113, pp. 429–434. Elsevier (2017)
22. Mansour, E., Chbeir, R., Arnould, P.: HSSN: an ontology for hybrid semantic sensor networks. In: Proceedings of the 23rd International Database Applications & Engineering Symposium, pp. 1–10 (2019)
23. Mansour, E., Chbeir, R., Arnould, P.: HSSN: an ontology for hybrid semantic sensor networks. In: Desai, B.C., Anagnostopoulos, D., Manolopoulos, Y., Nikolaidou, M. (eds.) Proceedings of the 23rd International Database Applications & Engineering Symposium, IDEAS 2019, Athens, Greece, 10–12 June 2019, pp. 8:1–8:10. ACM (2019). https://doi.org/10.1145/3331076.3331102
24. Mansour, E., Chbeir, R., Arnould, P., Allani, S., Salameh, K.: Data management in connected environments. Computing **103**(6), 1121–1142 (2021). https://doi.org/10.1007/s00607-020-00884-9

25. Mansour, E., Shahzad, F., Tekli, J., Chbeir, R.: Data redundancy management for leaf-edges in connected environments. Computing **104**(7), 1565–1588 (2022). https://doi.org/10.1007/s00607-021-01051-4
26. Marjani, M., et al.: Big IoT data analytics: architecture, opportunities, and open research challenges. IEEE Access **5**, 5247–5261 (2017)
27. Mehdipour, F., Javadi, B., Mahanti, A.: FOG-engine: towards big data analytics in the fog. In: 2016 IEEE 14th International Conference on Dependable, Autonomic and Secure Computing, Auckland, New Zealand, 8–12 August 2016, pp. 640–646. IEEE Computer Society (2016)
28. Montori, F., Bedogni, L., Bononi, L.: A collaborative internet of things architecture for smart cities and environmental monitoring. IEEE Internet Things J. **5**(2), 592–605 (2018)
29. Mozafari, B., et al.: SnappyData: a unified cluster for streaming, transactions and interactice analytics. In: CIDR 2017, 8th Biennial Conference on Innovative Data Systems Research, Chaminade, CA, USA, 8–11 January 2017, Online Proceedings (2017). www.cidrdb.org
30. Osman, A.M.S.: A novel big data analytics framework for smart cities. Future Gener. Comput. Syst. **91**, 620–633 (2019)
31. Park, J.H., Salim, M.M., Jo, J.H., Sicato, J.C.S., Rathore, S., Park, J.H.: CIoT-Net: a scalable cognitive IoT based smart city network architecture. Hum.-centric Comput. Inf. Sci. **9**, 29 (2019)
32. Sasaki, Y.: A survey on IoT big data analytic systems: current and future. IEEE Internet Things J. **9**(2), 1024–1036 (2022)
33. Sassi, M.S.H., Jedidi, F.G., Fourati, L.C.: A new architecture for cognitive internet of things and big data. In: Rudas, I.J., Csirik, J., Toro, C., Botzheim, J., Howlett, R.J., Jain, L.C. (eds.) Knowledge-Based and Intelligent Information & Engineering Systems: Proceedings of the 23rd International Conference KES-2019, Budapest, Hungary, 4–6 September 2019. Procedia Computer Science, vol. 159, pp. 534–543. Elsevier (2019)
34. Sezer, O.B., Dogdu, E., Ozbayoglu, A.M., Onal, A.: An extended IoT framework with semantics, big data, and analytics. In: Joshi, J., et al. (eds.) 2016 IEEE International Conference on Big Data (IEEE BigData 2016), Washington DC, USA, 5–8 December 2016, pp. 1849–1856. IEEE Computer Society (2016)
35. Siow, E., Tiropanis, T., Hall, W.: Analytics for the internet of things: a survey. ACM Comput. Surv. **51**(4), 74:1-74:36 (2018)
36. Sohail, I., Mahmood, T., Morshed, A., Sellis, T.: Big data analytics in healthcare - a systematic literature review and roadmap for practical implementation. IEEE CAA J. Autom. Sinica **8**(1), 1–22 (2021)
37. Stripelis, D., Ambite, J.L., Chiang, Y., Eckel, S.P., Habre, R.: A scalable data integration and analysis architecture for sensor data of pediatric asthma. In: 33rd IEEE International Conference on Data Engineering, ICDE 2017, San Diego, CA, USA, 19–22 April 2017, pp. 1407–1408. IEEE Computer Society (2017)
38. Wilcox, T., Jin, N., Flach, P.A., Thumim, J.: A big data platform for smart meter data analytics. Comput. Ind. **105**, 250–259 (2019)
39. Yassine, A., Singh, S., Hossain, M.S., Muhammad, G.: IoT big data analytics for smart homes with fog and cloud computing. Future Gener. Comput. Syst. **91**, 563–573 (2019)
40. Zhang, Q., Zhang, Q., Shi, W., Zhong, H.: Firework: data processing and sharing for hybrid cloud-edge analytics. IEEE Trans. Parallel Distrib. Syst. **29**(9), 2004–2017 (2018)

41. Zhu, L., Yu, F.R., Wang, Y., Ning, B., Tang, T.: Big data analytics in intelligent transportation systems: a survey. IEEE Trans. Intell. Transp. Syst. **20**(1), 383–398 (2019)

Knowledge Graph Augmentation for Increased Question Answering Accuracy

Jorge Martinez-Gil[1]($\boxtimes$), Shaoyi Yin[2], Josef Küng[3], and Franck Morvan[2]

[1] Software Competence Center Hagenberg GmbH,
Softwarepark 32a, 4232 Hagenberg, Austria
`jorge.martinez-gil@scch.at`
[2] Paul Sabatier University, IRIT Laboratory,
118 route de Narbonne, Toulouse, France
{`shaoyi.yin,franck.morvan`}`@irit.fr`
[3] Johannes Kepler University Linz,
Altenbergerstraße 69, 4040 Linz, Austria
`josef.kueng@jku.at`

Abstract. This research work presents a new augmentation model for knowledge graphs (KGs) that increases the accuracy of knowledge graph question answering (KGQA) systems. In the current situation, large KGs can represent millions of facts. However, the many nuances of human language mean that the answer to a given question cannot be found, or it is not possible to find always correct results. Frequently, this problem occurs because how the question is formulated does not fit with the information represented in the KG. Therefore, KGQA systems need to be improved to address this problem. We present a suite of augmentation techniques so that a wide variety of KGs can be automatically augmented, thus increasing the chances of finding the correct answer to a question. The first results from an extensive empirical study seem to be promising.

Keywords: Expert systems · Knowledge Engineering · Knowledge Graphs · Question Answering

1 Introduction

One of the most widely used representations of Knowledge Bases (KBs) is in the form of Knowledge Graphs (KGs). The nodes represent entities connected by relations in the form of a directed acyclic graph (DAG). Extensive research in the past decade has shown that these KGs can be extremely useful for many-core language tasks due to their simplistic structure and the ability to abstract facts and knowledge. Some disciplines that can benefit from KGs are question answering (QA) [12], recommender systems [10], etc.

© Springer-Verlag GmbH Germany, part of Springer Nature 2022
A. Hameurlain and A. M. Tjoa (Eds.): *Transactions on Large-Scale Data- and Knowledge-Centered Systems LII*, LNCS 13470, pp. 70–85, 2022.
https://doi.org/10.1007/978-3-662-66146-8_3

In the case of QA, many systems depend on a suitable KG to find proper answers, so there is little any QA system can do if the KG does not contain the answer. Thus, larger KGs generally lend to better QA performance unless the question domain is orthogonal to the KG [17]. In this way, having the correct information appear in many different forms reduces the burden on the QA system to perform complex operations to understand the text. However, to date, this research direction has been little explored.

In the context of QA systems, chatbots, or voice assistants, one of the most usual ways of operating consists of using a KG (e.g., Wikidata) to be queried (e.g., using SPARQL) to find the correct answer to a given question [7]. The question can even be supplemented with synonyms to help users ask the same question differently [1]. The problem is that the question reformulation in different ways is always executed on the same structural model. If the answer structure the QA system is looking for is not in the KG, all attempts are futile.

For this reason, data augmentation strategies can be proposed. The problem is that data augmentation for explicitly graph-structured data is still in its early stages [26]. Our proposal represents one of the first solutions in this direction. The Wikidata KG is automatically augmented to significantly increase the chances of finding an answer for any query reformulations. In addition, our strategy applies to any KG developed under the Resource Description Framework (RDF) umbrella, where knowledge is represented through facts very close to natural language. Therefore, we aim to facilitate the development of better quality KGs in an automated way, at least from the QA viewpoint.

As a result, the main contributions of this research work can be summarized as follows:

- We present a new augmentation model for KGs intended to improve the performance of KGs for QA. Our strategy is based on several levels of augmentation that considerably reduce the possibility of false positives during the process.
- We empirically evaluate such a strategy to establish the corresponding improvements over baseline methods.

The rest of this paper is structured as follows: Sect. 2 presents the state-of-the-art in knowledge graphs augmentation. Section 3 presents the technical details of our contribution. Section 4 reports the empirical study to which we have subjected our strategy and compares it with baseline strategies. Furthermore, we end with conclusions and lessons that can be learned from this research work.

2   Related Works

Currently, the use of KGs is widespread since they are beneficial in computational disciplines that require the use and exploitation of background knowledge to develop their tasks. Since integrating heterogeneous sources has improved as computer and communication technology has advanced, the amount of background knowledge generated increases and changes continuously. New techniques based on neural computation are the most popular for implementing QA systems. However, in the literature, we see that neural approaches often lack the background knowledge to complete some of their tasks. In recent times, there has been some agreement in the community that this background knowledge is highly desirable. Furthermore, it has been proved that this background knowledge can be effectively represented in a structured form like fact triplets [21].

Therefore, it seems clear that background knowledge can help in new domains, especially when crucial external information is needed. However, little has been done to augment KGs directly [3]. Instead, the research on KGs mainly focuses on three open issues: KG representation, KG construction, and KG application, which integrates many computer-related disciplines such as knowledge representation, information retrieval, and natural language processing. For this reason, our work presents as a novelty, an exploration of the KG augmentation to increase the efficiency and reliability of QA systems.

The rest of this section is structured as follows. Subsection 2.1 sets out the current state of the art concerning QA. Subsection 2.2 discusses QA systems using KGs. Subsection 2.3 explains why current methods for Query Expansion are often not good enough to find the proper answers. Subsection 2.4 explains how augmentation techniques come to fill this gap. Finally, in Subsect. 2.5, we explain the significant differences between augmentation and auto-completion and clarify how our research is positioned in the current state-of-the-art.

2.1   Question Answering

QA has been successfully applied in several domains, such as search engines and voice assistants. The reason is that QA can facilitate applications to access knowledge effectively. QA systems are generally considered collections of interconnected components, usually, through a pipeline, that automatically analyze various data sources in order to answer questions [19]. Building successful QA systems is considered challenging due to the inherent problems in managing considerable amounts of data [11]. In recent times, QA systems have become prevalent as opposed to systems that rely on ranking methods to provide different resources to find information related to a question [15].

The development of QA systems involves many and varied problems [8]. However, in this work, we focus on the problem of data redundancy. The notion of data redundancy in massive collections, such as large textual corpora, means that information is likely to be phrased in just one of the many ways it would be possible.

Finally, it is essential to emphasize that we are only concerned with KGQA systems in this research work. This means we are interested in QA systems aiming to exploit KGs, which store facts about the world in a structured format. This kind of system has become very popular recently due to the good results they can achieve compared to classic unstructured text-based systems [2].

2.2   Question Answering over Knowledge Graphs

Question Answering over Knowledge Graphs (KGQA) aims to find answers for natural language questions over a KG [27]. Recent KGQA approaches adopt a neural machine translation approach, where the natural language question is translated into a structured query language [24].

The main difficulty comes from the nature of human language and the fact that text suffers from ambiguity in most cases. In addition, sentences and questions about the same topic and case can be formulated differently [18]. Language is very dynamic, and people can ask a question in almost infinite different ways. So, in most cases, specifying and providing a precise answer to a question is complicated.

KGQA systems are intended to convert a question into a query to a given KG, thus avoiding the need to learn a graph-oriented query language [25]. However, an insufficient amount of data is typical when exploiting current KGs. This is because collecting such amount of data can be tedious and error-prone. An effective way to work with KGs that are not large enough is to reformulate the original query by adding some synonyms to expand the search space to find a suitable answer. However, as we will see below, these methods also have some disadvantages.

2.3   Insufficiency of Solutions for Query Expansion

One of the most popular methods in the QA domain is query expansion. Query expansion tries to augment a search query with other terms such as relevant synonyms or semantically related terms [5,20]. This process is widely used in information retrieval systems to improve the results and increase recall [28]. Users either ask questions with minimal keywords that do not reflect the user intention or are inexperienced in the topic they are searching for. Therefore, query expansion is done assuming that the structure of the user query reflects the user's real intention. Moreover, the chance of finding a meaningful answer is low if no standard form is shared between the original question and how the knowledge is represented in the KG. Therefore, exploring methods to augment KGs automatically and without structural constraints seems reasonable.

2.4   Data Augmentation

Data Augmentation (DA) is a set of techniques that can be used to artificially expand the size of a dataset by creating modified data from the existing one [9]. For example, in the machine learning field, it is usually good to use DA to prevent overfitting or when the initial dataset is too small to train on or achieve better performance. In this way, DA is crucial for many applications as accuracy increases with available data.

It is widely assumed that DA can significantly improve tasks such as classification and segmentation accuracy in many domains. However, the use of DA techniques regarding KGs is little explored. In the context of KGs, DA can be formally defined as

$$D \leftarrow (D, D_{aug}), D_{aug} \leftarrow \{ (o, p_r, s) \mid \forall x \in D, x = (s, p, o)\}$$

Although there are some precedents, DA is not as popular in working with textual information as in other domains. The reason is that augmenting textual data is challenging due to the nuances of the natural language [13]. In this way, generating new data samples is one way to augment existing data, but there is a high risk of creating incorrect knowledge. However, there are other safer approaches (e.g., minor changes to existing data, deterministic transformations, and so on) for DA.

2.5 Differences Between KG Augmentation and KG Auto-Completion

Most existing approaches use some methods for auto-completion of KGs [4]. This task is usually called KG auto-completion. It extensively focuses on tackling this issue by learning models, commonly known as link predictors, that can complete any fact with partial information. More recently, neural network-based methods, commonly called neural link predictors, have become state-of-the-art for KG completion tasks. However, since these models are supervised learners, their ability is directly tied to the available training data.

Moreover, in KG auto-completion, the aim is to complete a fact, e.g., *(Socrates, is-a, ?)*. KG augmentation does not try to guess unknown information. However, it starts from the idea of making changes to the existing facts, e.g., *(Socrates, is-a, philosopher)* → *(Socrates, is-a, thinker), (Socrates, was-a, philosopher), (philosophy, is-contributed-by, Socrates), (Socrates, was-a, classic thinker)*, etc. While KG auto-completion is a machine learning challenge subject to much uncertainty, KG augmentation is a data management challenge. It is much more deterministic, preserving knowledge by minimizing the possibility of making serious errors. At the same time, it facilitates the accommodation of different formulations of a question only at the expense of needing more secondary memory (which is currently relatively cheap).

In this work, we adopt an approach based on KG augmentation. KG augmentation aims to expand the data sources to be analyzed to improve the limits of existing KGs. This strategy allows leveraging vast volumes of data to provide insights, forecasts, and suggestions previously unattainable owing to a lack of relevant data, even if starting with very little [29].

2.6 Positioning in the State-of-the-Art

Much research work has been devoted to KG auto-completion. A common approach is KG embedding, representing entities and relations in triples as real-valued vectors and assessing triples' plausibility with these vectors. However, most KG embedding models only use structure information in observed triple facts. Furthermore, syntactic and semantic information in large-scale data is not fully utilized, as KG embeddings only employ entity descriptions, relation mentions, or word co-occurrence with entities [30]. Our research shows for the first time a strategy for KG augmentation that improves the quality of KGQA systems thanks to the automatic enrichment of the knowledge contained in the KG. To do this, we will try to make changes that are not too intrusive to save the veracity of the represented knowledge.

Our approach should be helpful in open-domain QA. For example, when dealing with factoid questions over KGs. A standard practice to execute a query using SPARQL over the KG to extract answer entities. Query expansion for this purpose adds a layer of difficulty. Our hypothesis is that a fully augmented KG might facilitate finding the correct answers by being much more flexible in allowing different formulations of the same or closely-related question.

3 Automatic Knowledge Graph Augmentation

Although QA systems are valuable and sought in various fields, developing efficient ways for assessing questions and determining responses is a difficult challenge. The fundamental challenge stems from the nature of human language and the fact that most texts can be reformulated without loss. Furthermore, questions concerning the same topic and instance might be phrased differently. People can ask a question in an almost limitless number of different ways. As a result, defining and providing a specific answer to a question is complex. Automatic KG augmentation can substantially reduce human effort and ensures the quality of machine-generated data using the results of performance improvements. It can also extend the relational information of given concept sets, including additional knowledge for the intended input query.

We can define a Knowledge Graph $\mathcal{KG} = \{(sub, pred, obj)\} \subseteq \mathcal{E} \times \mathcal{R} \times \mathcal{E}$ as a set of triples of the form $(sub, pred, obj)$ such that $sub \in \mathcal{E}$, $pred \in \mathcal{R}$ and $obj \in \mathcal{E}$. In this way, $\mathcal{E}$ and $\mathcal{R}$ are the sets of all entities and relation types of $\mathcal{KG}$.

Figure 1 shows an example of a KG in which facts in the form of subject, predicate, and object are modeled to give rise to a DAG that semantically models information.

For a given $\mathcal{KG} = \{(\mathcal{V}, \mathcal{E}, \mathcal{X})\}$ where $\mathcal{V}$ is a set containing $|\mathcal{V}|$ nodes, $\mathcal{E}$ is the set of edges showing the links between nodes, and $\mathcal{X}$ is the attribute matrix. A KG augmentation $Aug(\cdot)$ aims to learn a mapping function $\Phi : \Phi(\mathcal{V}, \mathcal{E}, \mathcal{X}) \mapsto \mathcal{R}^{|\mathcal{V}| \cdot \mathcal{V}}$ that projects graph nodes to d dimension latent representation $\mathcal{Z}$, where $\Phi : Aug(\Phi')$ being Φ' the mapping function.

While it is true that, in graph-oriented queries, the essential nodes are usually extended with synonymous words to facilitate cases where users set the question in different forms, we have adopted a radically different approach in this work that overcome specific weaknesses, e.g., safe creation of new fact triplets. KG augmentation is a set of methods to artificially increase the size of a KG by generating new facts from existing data. This includes making minor changes to data or using heuristics to generate new facts [29]. KG applications, especially in data and knowledge engineering, continue to increase quickly. KG augmentation

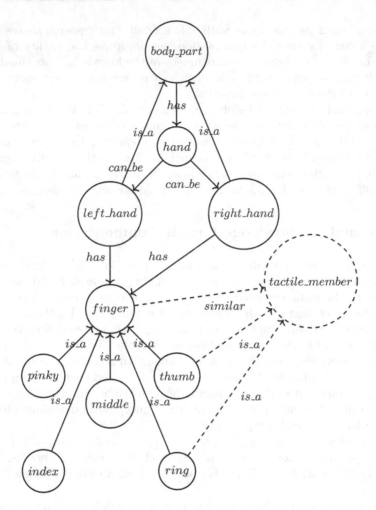

Fig. 1. Example of a Knowledge Graph representing some general-purpose knowledge. It consists of 12 fact triplets of type (subject, predicate, object). It can be easily and safely augmented with new facts that facilitates the answering of more questions. For example: (finger, equivalent, tactile_member), (ring, is_a, tactile_member), (thumb, is_a, tactile_member), etc. Such augmentation will be only at the expense of increased secondary memory consumption.

techniques may be an excellent tool to face the community's challenges. Manually curating and extending existing KG can lead to exhausting, error-prone, and costly processes. Transformations in KGs using augmentation techniques allow for reducing these operational costs. In this way, augmentation techniques make KGs more complete by creating diverse variations, and therefore, they facilitate finding the correct answer to a given question.

In this work, we consider four types of augmentation covering lexical, syntactic, and semantic aspects:

- Character-level augmentation
- Item-level augmentation
- Component-level augmentation
- An efficient combination of all of them

We will now explain each of them in detail. Subsequently, we will undertake an empirical evaluation that will allow us to explore the strengths and weaknesses of each of them.

3.1 Character-Level Augmentation

Character-level augmentation has been widely used because the augmentation mechanism is straightforward to realize. Compared to other augmentation strategies, these augmentation strategies generally have lower computational costs but can also achieve decent accuracy. Since such an augmentation strategy function does not consider graph structures, it can be used in large graphs. Accordingly, it has broader applications than the other strategies and can effectively improve the reliability of the KGQA systems.

The rationale behind this strategy is that variability is inherent to the human language. Therefore, this kind of KG augmentation can be understood as a way to proceed with a lemmatization process, determining the root of the words to prevent irregular forms (i.e., plurals, third persons, and so on).

3.2 Item-Level Augmentation

In order to enhance graph representation, item-level augmentation techniques generally employ information on target nodes and edges. Compared with character level augmentation, these techniques pay attention to the nodes in the graph. The universality is weaker than that of character-level strategies. Consequently, this strategy is more prevalent in recommendation systems and neural language processing. The most popular techniques in this category are synonym replacement, random token insertion, and random token deletion. Please note that this method is never applied to proper nouns because they usually have no substitute.

Synonym Replacement. It randomly chooses words from the subject or object that do not stop words. Replace each of these words with one of its synonyms selected at random. In order to do that, it should be possible to use word2vec [22] or contextual embeddings like BERT [6]. Dictionaries can also be used to find synonyms for the desired token from the original entity that must be replaced. The popular WordNet [23] is an example of a resource to be used here.

Random Token Insertion. It consists of inserting a random word into the entity. Nevertheless, it is assumed that this insertion should not be a stop word. For these random insertions to make sense, they must be supported by a contextual embedding solution such as BERT [6], which can predict the words that usually appear next to a given one.

Random Token Deletion. It consists of deleting a random word into the entity. It is assumed that the deletion should not be a stop word. For random deletion to make sense, it is preferable to proceed with adverbs or adjectives since they carry less semantic load than nouns.

3.3 Component-Level Augmentation

It consists of working on the level of a complete fact (subject, predicate, object). The most popular techniques in this category are: swapping and structure prediction.

Swapping. It consists of choosing the subject and the object in the triplet and swapping their positions. In addition, the predicate must be adapted accordingly through a reversal operation. This operation is prevalent since it enables semantic swaps that preserve the global consistency [13].

Structure Prediction. Structured language in graph form helps achieve this augmentation capability. It can be done using any KG-auto completion technique since we will not rely on information already expressed.

3.4 An Efficient Combination of All of Them

In augmentation research, a common technique combines several KG augmentation methods to achieve more diversified instances. Here, the combination can mean applying multiple separate or stacked methods. In this way, while the results of the two augmentation methods might differ significantly, combining both methods should produce good results.

It is essential to note that some combinations may be safer than others in preserving knowledge. For example, a reasonably safe combination can be made by choosing one type of augmentation from each branch, such that (*philosophers, like, reading*) could be replaced by (*read*, is-liked, thinkers*). It can be seen how a character-level, synonym replacement, and swapping have been performed, respectively. The massive insertion of these triplets helps accommodate possible human operator queries. In addition, there is always the possibility of using more aggressive strategies if the original question cannot be satisfied. For example (*thinkers, enjoy, reading books*) whereby two synonym replacements and one random insertion have been considered.

4   Results

This section presents our results after subjecting our proposal to an extensive empirical study. So first, we describe the datasets we are going to work with. The configuration we have selected to perform the experiments, the empirical results we have obtained for the different variants of our strategy, and their appropriate comparison with baseline methods. Then, we show an empirical study on our performance when testing the strategy. Finally, we discuss the results we have obtained.

4.1 Datasets

The KG that we will use as a base to be augmented will be Wikidata[1]. This corpus consists of the entire Wikidata KG, and it takes 33 GB, approx. Although this is due to overhead, the amount of net data is significantly lower. At the same time, we have chosen some questionnaires (i.e., adapted pairs of questions and answers) on geography and history, which have been taken from a subset of the popular OpenTrivia benchmark dataset [14]. The reason for choosing this dataset is that it contains primarily questions in factoid format, which in principle, is the most suitable format expected for a KGQA-based system. Nevertheless, since ours is a general-purpose framework, there would be no restriction to operating on other single-response datasets.

4.2 Setup

The configuration we have chosen is as follows:

- *Character level*, we have chosen the Krovetz solution [16].
- *Item Level - Synonym Replacement*, using the synonyms ranked first in Wordnet.
- *Item Level - Random Insertion*, using the first prediction of BERT.
- *Item Level - Random Deletion*, a token is erased randomly when the entity has more than one token.
- *Component-level - Swapping*, subject and object are interchanged, and the predicate is switched to passive voice.
- *Component Level - Structure prediction*, calculated with TransE from the Ampligraph library[2]
- *An efficient combination of all of them*, we calculate all possible permutations, choosing one method from each of the three families at each iteration. We report only the best result.

There is one crucial thing to keep in mind at this point. Augmentation techniques may or may not be associated with worse results than baseline. For example, work with the augmented copies only to find answers to questions not satisfied by the original KG. The result will never be inferior to the baseline. However, running the program will require much more time since it has to navigate between several augmented copies. Nevertheless, in no case will the human operator get worse results.

In another case, the queries are performed directly on the augmented KG to check if they can be satisfied. In these cases, the execution time will be very

---

[1] https://www.wikidata.org/.
[2] https://github.com/Accenture/AmpliGraph/.

similar (although it depends significantly on the degree of augmentation of the original KG). However, it is quite true that the results may vary significantly concerning the baseline.

In this work, we take as a form of evaluation the first one. The answers are sought in augmented copies of the KG only if they could not be satisfied initially.

4.3   Empirical Evaluation

Below, we show our results after submitting our different strategies to an empirical evaluation. The baseline consists of using the original Wikidata KG. Furthermore, each of the following strategies works on the original Wikidata KG to check if such augmentation can facilitate better results. We also show the augmentation factor, which means the amount of memory space required to store the augmented KG, being 1.00 the original Wikidata KG.

Table 1 shows the results for the questions on general geography. Sometimes it is challenging to know specific data about geography. We now want to see if our proposal could help a human operator satisfactorily.

Table 1. Results for the subset of general geography from OpenTrivia

Method	Score
Baseline (Original Wikidata)	0.57
Augm-Character Level - Krovetz Lemmatization	0.62
Augm-Item Level - Synonym Replacement	0.66
Augm-Item Level - Random Insertion	0.57
Augm-Item Level - Random Deletion	0.47
Augm-Component Level - Swapping	0.57
Augm-Component Level - Structure prediction	0.62
Augm-Smart Combination	**0.67**

Table 2 shows us the results on the questions about the history of humankind, regardless of date or geographical region. It is not easy for a human operator to store all this encyclopedic knowledge.

Table 3 shows us the augmentation factor, which means the amount of memory space required to store the augmented KG, being 1.00 the original Wikidata KG. Please note that we have taken a conservative approach. For example, in the case of swapping, three operations could be performed on subject, predicate and object respectively. However, to guarantee the preservation of knowledge, we have only performed on one permutation at a time.

Table 2. Results for the subset of general history from OpenTrivia

Method	Score
Baseline (Original Wikidata)	0.57
Augm-Character Level - Krovetz Lemmatization	0.62
Augm-Item Level - Synonym Replacement	0.66
Augm-Item Level - Random Insertion	0.57
Augm-Item Level - Random Deletion	0.46
Augm-Component Level - Swapping	0.57
Augm-Component Level - Structure prediction	**0.71**
Augm-Smart Combination	0.70

Table 3. Size of the Wikidata KG after undergoing augmentation operation

Method	Aug.
Baseline (Original Wikidata)	1.00
Augm-Character Level - Krovetz Lemmatization	0.98
Augm-Item Level - Synonym Replacement	2.53
Augm-Item Level - Random Insertion	1.26
Augm-Item Level - Random Deletion	0.86
Augm-Component Level - Swapping	1.01
Augm-Component Level - Structure prediction	1.33
Augm-Smart Combination	1.77

4.4   Discussion

Methods and techniques for automatically answering questions are in high demand. As a result, many solutions for QA have been developed to respond to this need. In this context, building models that seamlessly handle structured data (e.g., KG) has been a long-sought-after goal. The reason is that KGs allow overcoming limitations about the structure and semantics of the information they represent. We have seen how the research community has proposed efficient methodologies for analyzing questions and specifying proper answers using KGs with quite reasonable returns. In this way, the advantages inherent in the use of KG in contexts, such as the one we are dealing with here, can be summarized as follows:

- Improving KGQA accuracy by safely adding more data into the KGs
- Reducing costs of manually augmenting the KGs
- Facilitating answers to rare questions
- Preventing privacy issues (if needed)

The main issue faced when working with augmented KGs is that the model may need much more computation time to find no answer. Most KG augmentation learning methods focus on homogeneous graphs, including augmenting nodes, structural attributes, or models. However, the continuous development of KG learning methods is still difficult to handle the problem of heterogeneity in graph data. For this reason, we will now list the lessons we have learned from this research work:

– It is always possible to try different augmentation approaches and check which works better
– An aggregation of different augmentation methods is also a good idea
– It is possible to determine the optimal method combination for the best results
– Data augmentation in KGs does not always help to improve the performance

Furthermore, KG augmentation can be beneficial for increasing the accuracy of KGQAs. However, it does lead to an increase in the use of secondary memory. Nevertheless, this type of memory does not usually represent a high cost in recent times. In addition, it would be possible to look for data management techniques that optimize the consumption of resources. Furthermore, a possible strategy of combining techniques for query expansion and KG augmentation simultaneously could also help meet this challenge.

5   Conclusions

QA systems have become more critical than ever in recent years. The main reasons are the ongoing expansion in the available information and the necessity to help people get the information they need precisely, quickly, and efficiently. We have seen how KG augmentation is crucial for building more accurate and robust KGs. An appropriate pre-processing with data augmentation can help build state-of-the-art systems.

This research has presented our approach to using natural language generation for data-centric research to reduce the cost of leveraging building an augmented KG. Automatic knowledge augmentation for KGQA systems is not limited to a particular model but can be applied in different forms. Our approach demonstrates the positive effects of KG augmentation through comparative experiments using datasets belonging to different domains. Moreover, some guidelines for suitable and feasible KG augmentation strategies have been provided.

In future work, the community must consider the necessity to develop evaluation methodologies for measuring the quality of augmented KGs. As the use of augmentation methods increases, assessing their quality will be required. It is also important to consider that if an actual KG has biases, a KG augmented from it will also have those biases. So, the identification of a good KG augmentation approach is essential.

Furthermore, it is also necessary to consider that augmentation models are generally time-consuming and have some space complexity. As the number of nodes or edges increases in large-scale graphs, the augmentation factor will also increase. Nevertheless, until now, there has been no effective parallel solution for handling this issue. The problem of high cost, the selection of augmentation strategy, and the optimization of the augmentation model are the main problems that need to be faced in the future.

Acknowledgements. The authors thank the anonymous reviewers for their help in improving the work. This work has been supported by the Austrian Ministry for Transport, Innovation and Technology, the Federal Ministry of Science, Research and Economy, and the State of Upper Austria through the COMET center SCCH. And by the project FR06/2020 - International Cooperation & Mobility (ICM) of the Austrian Agency for International Cooperation in Education and Research (OeAD-GmbH). We would also thank 'the French Ministry of Foreign and European Affairs' and 'The French Ministry of Higher Education and Research' which support the Amadeus program 2020 (French-Austrian Hubert Curien Partnership - PHC) Project Number 44086TD.

References

1. Azad, H.K., Deepak, A.: Query expansion techniques for information retrieval: a survey. Inf. Process. Manag. **56**(5), 1698–1735 (2019)
2. Berant, J., Chou, A., Frostig, R., Liang, P.: Semantic parsing on freebase from question-answer pairs. In: Proceedings of the 2013 Conference on Empirical Methods in Natural Language Processing, EMNLP 2013, 18–21 October 2013, Grand Hyatt Seattle, Seattle, Washington, USA, A meeting of SIGDAT, a Special Interest Group of the ACL, pp. 1533–1544. ACL (2013)
3. Cannaviccio, M., Ariemma, L., Barbosa, D., Merialdo, P.: Leveraging wikipedia table schemas for knowledge graph augmentation. In Proceedings of the 21st International Workshop on the Web and Databases, Houston, TX, USA, 10 June 2018, pp. 5:1–5:6. ACM (2018)
4. Chen, Z., Wang, Y., Zhao, B., Cheng, J., Zhao, X., Duan, Z.: Knowledge graph completion: a review. IEEE Access **8**, 192435–192456 (2020)
5. Deerwester, S.C., Dumais, S.T., Landauer, T.K., Furnas, G.W., Harshman, R.A.: Indexing by latent semantic analysis. J. Am. Soc. Inf. Sci. **41**(6), 391–407 (1990)
6. Devlin, J., Chang, M.-W., Lee, K., Toutanova, K.: Bert: pre-training of deep bidirectional transformers for language understanding. arXiv preprint arXiv:1810.04805 (2018)
7. Diefenbach, D., Tanon, T.P., Singh, K.D., Maret, P.: Question answering benchmarks for wikidata. In: Nikitina, N., Song, D., Fokoue, A., Haase, P. (eds.), Proceedings of the ISWC 2017 Posters & Demonstrations and Industry Tracks colocated with 16th International Semantic Web Conference (ISWC 2017), Vienna, Austria, 23rd - to - 25th October 2017, vol. 1963 of CEUR Workshop Proceedings, CEUR-WS.org (2017)
8. Dimitrakis, E., Sgontzos, K., Tzitzikas, Y.: A survey on question answering systems over linked data and documents. J. Intell. Inf. Syst. **55**(2), 233–259 (2019). https://doi.org/10.1007/s10844-019-00584-7
9. Feng, S.Y., et al.: A survey of data augmentation approaches for NLP. In: Zong, C., Xia, F., Li, W., Navigli, R. (eds.), Findings of the Association for Computational Linguistics: ACL/IJCNLP 2021, Online Event, 1–6 August 2021, vol. ACL/IJCNLP 2021 of Findings of ACL, pp. 968–988. Association for Computational Linguistics (2021)

10. Guo, Q., et al.: A survey on knowledge graph-based recommender systems. IEEE Trans. Knowl. Data Eng. **34**(8), 3549–3568 (2020)
11. Hameurlain, A., Morvan, F.: Big data management in the cloud: evolution or crossroad? In: Kozielski, S., Mrozek, D., Kasprowski, P., Małysiak-Mrozek, B., Kostrzewa, D. (eds.) BDAS 2015-2016. CCIS, vol. 613, pp. 23–38. Springer, Cham (2016). https://doi.org/10.1007/978-3-319-34099-9_2
12. Hirschman, L., Gaizauskas, R.J.: Natural language question answering: the view from here. Nat. Lang. Eng. **7**(4), 275–300 (2001)
13. Huang, L., Wu, L., Wang, L.: Knowledge graph-augmented abstractive summarization with semantic-driven cloze reward. In: Jurafsky, D., Chai, J., Schluter, N., Tetreault, J.R. (eds.), Proceedings of the 58th Annual Meeting of the Association for Computational Linguistics, ACL 2020, Online, 5–10 July 2020, pp. 5094–5107. Association for Computational Linguistics (2020)
14. Joshi, M., Choi, E., Weld, D.S., Zettlemoyer, L.: Triviaqa: a large scale distantly supervised challenge dataset for reading comprehension. In: Proceedings of the 55th Annual Meeting of the Association for Computational Linguistics (Volume 1: Long Papers), pp. 1601–1611 (2017)
15. Kolomiyets, O., Moens, M.: A survey on question answering technology from an information retrieval perspective. Inf. Sci. **181**(24), 5412–5434 (2011)
16. Krovetz, R.: Viewing morphology as an inference process. Artif. Intell. **118**(1–2), 277–294 (2000)
17. Lan, Y., He, G., Jiang, J., Jiang, J., Zhao, W.X., Wen, J.: A survey on complex knowledge base question answering: methods, challenges and solutions. In: Zhou, Z. (eds.), Proceedings of the Thirtieth International Joint Conference on Artificial Intelligence, IJCAI 2021, Virtual Event/Montreal, Canada, 19–27 August 2021, pp. 4483–4491. ijcai.org (2021)
18. Martinez-Gil, J., Chaves-Gonzalez, J.M.: Semantic similarity controllers: on the trade-off between accuracy and interpretability. Knowl.-Based Syst. **234**, 107609 (2021)
19. Martinez-Gil, J., Freudenthaler, B., Tjoa, A.M.: A general framework for multiple choice question answering based on mutual information and reinforced co-occurrence. Trans. Large Scale Data Knowl. Centered Syst. **42**, 91–110 (2019)
20. Martinez-Gil, J., Mokadem, R., Küng, J., Hameurlain, A.: A novel Neurofuzzy approach for semantic similarity measurement. In: Golfarelli, M., Wrembel, R., Kotsis, G., Tjoa, A.M., Khalil, I. (eds.) DaWaK 2021. LNCS, vol. 12925, pp. 192–203. Springer, Cham (2021). https://doi.org/10.1007/978-3-030-86534-4_18
21. Martinez-Gil, J., Mokadem, R., Morvan, F., Küng, J., Hameurlain, A.: Interpretable entity meta-alignment in knowledge graphs using penalized regression: a case study in the biomedical domain. Prog. Artif. Intell. **11**(1), 93–104 (2022)
22. Mikolov, T., Sutskever, I., Chen, K., Corrado, G.S., Dean, J.: Distributed representations of words and phrases and their compositionality. In: Advances in Neural Information Processing Systems 26: 27th Annual Conference on Neural Information Processing Systems 2013, Proceedings of a meeting held 5–8 December 2013, Lake Tahoe, Nevada, United States, pp. 3111–3119 (2013)
23. Miller, G.A.: wordnet: a lexical database for English. Commun. ACM **38**(11), 39–41 (1995)
24. Perevalov, A., Diefenbach, D., Usbeck, R., Both, A.: Qald-9-plus: a multilingual dataset for question answering over dbpedia and wikidata translated by native speakers. In: 16th IEEE International Conference on Semantic Computing, ICSC 2022, Laguna Hills, CA, USA, 26–28 January 2022, pp. 229–234. IEEE (2022)

25. Ploumis, T., Perikos, I., Grivokostopoulou, F., Hatzilygeroudis, I.: A factoid based question answering system based on dependency analysis and wikidata. In: Bourbakis, N.G., Tsihrintzis, G.A., Virvou, M. (eds.), 12th International Conference on Information, Intelligence, Systems & Applications, IISA 2021, Chania Crete, Greece, 12–14 July 2021, pp. 1–7. IEEE (2021)
26. Shorten, C., Khoshgoftaar, T.M., Furht, B.: Text data augmentation for deep learning. J. Big Data **8**(1), 101 (2021)
27. Steinmetz, N., Sattler, K.: What is in the KGQA benchmark datasets? survey on challenges in datasets for question answering on knowledge graphs. J. Data Semant. **10**(3–4), 241–265 (2021)
28. Xiong, C., Callan, J.: Query expansion with freebase. In: Allan, J., Croft, W.B., de Vries, A.P., Zhai, C. (eds.), Proceedings of the 2015 International Conference on The Theory of Information Retrieval, ICTIR 2015, Northampton, Massachusetts, USA, 27–30 September 2015, pp. 111–120. ACM (2015)
29. Yu, S., Huang, H., Dao, M.N., Xia, F.: Graph augmentation learning. arXiv preprint arXiv:2203.09020 (2022)
30. Zhao, Z., Liu, T., Li, S., Li, B., Du, X.: Ngram2vec: learning improved word representations from ngram co-occurrence statistics. In: Palmer, M., Hwa, R., Riedel, S. (eds.), Proceedings of the 2017 Conference on Empirical Methods in Natural Language Processing, EMNLP 2017, Copenhagen, Denmark, 9–11 September 2017, pp. 244–253. Association for Computational Linguistics (2017)

Online Optimized Product Quantization for ANN Queries over Dynamic Database using SVD-Updating

Kota Yukawa[1] and Toshiyuki Amagasa[2]($\boxtimes$) (iD)

[1] Graduate School of Science and Technology, University of Tsukuba,
Tsukuba, Japan
yukawa@kde.cs.tsukuba.ac.jp
[2] Center for Computational Sciences, University of Tsukuba,
Tsukuba, Japan
amagasa@cs.tsukuba.ac.jp

Abstract. Approximate nearest neighbor (ANN) search allows us to perform similarity search over massive vectors with less memory and computation. Optimized Product Quantization (OPQ) is one of the state-of-the-art methods for ANN where data vectors are represented as combinations of codewords by taking into account the data distribution. However, it suffers from degradation in accuracy when the database is frequently updated with incoming data whose distribution is different. An existing work, Online OPQ, addressed this problem, but the computational cost is high because it requires to perform of costly singular value decomposition for updating the codewords. To this problem, we propose a method for updating the rotation matrix using SVD-Updating, which can dynamically update the singular matrix using low-rank approximation. Using SVD-Updating, instead of performing multiple singular value decomposition on a high-rank matrix, we can update the rotation matrix by performing only one singular value decomposition on a low-rank matrix. In the experiments, we prove that the proposed method shows a better trade-off between update time and retrieval accuracy than the comparative methods.

Keywords: ANN Search · Product Quantization · Online PQ

1 Introduction

The nearest neighbor (NN) search is a fundamental operation over a database whereby one can retrieve similar vectors for a given query vector. Besides, k-nearest neighbor (kNN) search outputs not only the nearest but also k ranked nearest neighbors. They are frequently used in a broad spectrum of applications, such as multimedia search over images, audio, or videos, and inside of machine learning algorithms as well.

© Springer-Verlag GmbH Germany, part of Springer Nature 2022
A. Hameurlain and A. M. Tjoa (Eds.): *Transactions on Large-Scale Data- and Knowledge-Centered Systems LII*, LNCS 13470, pp. 86–102, 2022.
https://doi.org/10.1007/978-3-662-66146-8_4

The computational complexity of the kNN search increases according to the dimensionality and the database's size being processed. More specifically, it requires $\mathcal{O}(ND)$ where D and N represent the dimensionality and the number of data, respectively. So, it is important to improve efficiency when dealing with high-dimensional data at scale. It should be noticed that, in a kNN search, we do not need the exact distances among vectors if the relative distances among vectors are well-preserved. To take advantage of this property, the approximate nearest neighbor (ANN) search is often used. The idea is to use approximated vectors so that we can quickly process kNN queries and save memory space as well.

The *product quantization (PQ)* [9] is one of the well-known methods for ANN search. In PQ, we divide each vector into some subvectors. Then, for the subvectors of the same subspace, we apply k-means clustering to quantize them. As a result, we can represent each vector as a combination of codewords corresponding to the cluster centroid, thereby significantly reducing data volume. Moreover, PQ has been shown to reduce the quantization error compared to conventional vector quantization because each vector is represented as a product of subvectors. PQ shows a good trade-off between accuracy/efficiency and memory cost. To improve the method, many variants have been published in recent years. The *optimized PQ (OPQ)* [7] introduces a vector space rotation as a pre-transformation to minimize the quantization error. OPQ can be done by mutually optimizing the optimal codebook and rotation matrix and successfully showed better accuracy than the original PQ.

Meanwhile, the number of real-time information sources has been drastically increasing due to the proliferation of network-attached devices. Therefore, there has been a growing demand for processing dynamic data, such as data streams [5,13]. The kNN search on such dynamic databases has been used in many applications, such as video search, and we can consider to apply PQ/OPQ to such data to get the benefits as discussed above. However, it gives rise to another problem – the codebook optimized for the existing data becomes obsolete gradually as new data arrives, resulting in search accuracy degradation. *Online PQ* [20] proposed dynamically updating the codebook for new data and showed efficiency in updating the codebook while maintaining the search accuracy. Besides, *Online Optimized PQ* [12] proposed dynamically updating the rotation matrix to adapt Optimized PQ to time series data. However, it requires costly singular value decomposition (SVD) when updating the rotation matrix, leading to a long time to update.

In this paper, we address the problem of improving the efficiency of Online Optimized PQ. More specifically, we update the codebook and rotation matrix by applying the singular value decomposition updating method called SVD-Updating [3], thereby reducing the updating cost of Online Optimized PQs. In SVD-Updating, the computational cost is reduced using the singular value decomposition of a low-rank approximation matrix instead of the singular value decomposition on a full-rank matrix. In addition, we propose a method using *sliding windows*, which are commonly used for querying streaming data. In our experiments, we use a total of three datasets, text and image. We prove that the proposed method shows a good trade-off between the two methods, maintaining almost the same accuracy with less model update time than existing methods.

The rest of this paper is organized as follows.

We introduce some preliminary concepts and definitions in Sect. 2, followed by making a literature review of the related work in Sect. 3. In Sect. 4, we will describe our proposed method and its performance will be tested by the expeimental evaluations in Sect. 5. Finally, Sect. 6 concludes this paper and mention our future works.

2   Preliminaries

2.1   Approximate K-Nearest Neighbor Search

Let us assume a set of vectors $X = \{x_0, \cdots, x_{N-1}\} \in \mathbb{R}^D$. Given a query vector $q \in \mathbb{R}^D$, the nearest neighbor (NN) search over X is defined as:

$$x* = argmin_{x \in X} \, dist(x, q) \tag{1}$$

where $dist(\cdot)$ is a distance measure. In the approximate NN (ANN) search, an approximated distance measure is used instead of the original one. Besides, in the k-NN (k-ANN) search, top k nearest vectors are retrieved.

2.2   Vector Quantization (VQ)

The idea of *Vector Quantization (VQ)* [8] is to approximate a vectors by a short representation called codeword, thereby reducing the space and time required to process them. More concretely, the distance between the query and data is approximated by the distance between the codewords corresponding to the query and the data. In the basic VQ, vectors $X = \{x_0, \cdots, x_{N-1}\} \in \mathbb{R}^D$ are clustered using the k-means method. Each clustered vector is approximated as a cluster centroid $C \in c_i (0 \leq i \leq k - 1)$. The cluster centroid c_i is called a codeword, and the set of cluster centroids C is called a codebook. The objective function of the codebook is to minimize the sum of squared errors, i.e.,

$$\min_C \sum_X \|x - c_i(x)\|^2 \tag{2}$$

2.3   Product Quantization (PQ)

The *Product Quantization (PQ)* [9] was proposed as an improved method. Each vector is divided into M subvectors of equal length:

$$x = x^1 \times \cdots \times x^M \tag{3}$$

Thus, any vector can be expressed as an element in the cartesian product of M sets of subvectors. Then, for each set of subvectors, we apply VQ to compress the subvectors. As a result, we can represent a vector in terms of M sub-codewords. The objective function for the codebook optimization is as follows:

$$\min_{C^1,\cdots,C^M} \sum_X \sum_{m=1}^M \|x^m - c_i^m(x^m)\|^2 \tag{4}$$
$$\text{s.t.} C = C^1 \times \cdots \times C^M$$

where x^m represents the m-th subvector of x, and $c_i^m(x^m)$ represents the i-th codeword corresponding to x^m. It has been proven that the quantization error of PQ is smaller than that of VQ, because each vector is represented as a Cartesian product of sub-codebooks.

2.4   Optimized PQ

The *Optimized Product Quantization (OPQ)* [7] was proposed to improve PQ. The idea is to reduce the quantization error by applying rotation to the dataset. To this end, they use a rotation matrix R in addition to the original PQ. The objective function for the rotation matrix and codebook optimization is:

$$\min_{R,C^1,\cdots,C^M} \sum_X \sum_{m=1}^M \|x^m - c_i^m(x^m)\|^2 \tag{5}$$
$$\text{s.t.} c \in C = \{c|Rc = C^1 \times \cdots \times C^M, R^T R\}$$

The optimal rotation matrix can be obtained by solving the orthogonal procrustes problem [15]. Therefore, the optimal rotation matrix can be obtained by using singular value decomposition as follows:

$$SVD(XC(X^T)) = USV^T$$
$$R = VU^T \tag{6}$$

To optimizes the rotation matrix and the codebook, they apply alternative optimization over the codebook and the rotation matrix.

2.5   Online PQ

When dealing with dynamic data where new vectors are continually added, the performance of PQ and OPQ gradually degrades, because the codebook is optimized to minimized for the set of vectors when the codebook is created while the distribution of incoming vectors may differ from the past dataset. To this problem, the *Online Product Quantization (Online PQ)* [20] retrains the codebook only by using the new vectors, thereby making it possible to adapt the codebook to the change in vector distribution. The objective function is:

$$\min_{C^{t,1},\cdots,C^{t,M}} \sum_{X} \sum_{m=1}^{M} \|x^{t,m} - c_i^{t,m}(x^{t,m})\|^2$$

$$\text{s.t.} C = C^{t,1} \times \cdots \times C^{t,M}$$

(7)

where $c_i^{t,m}(x^{t,m})$ is the nearest neighbor codeword corresponding to the input data $x^{t,m}$ in the m-th subspace of the t-th data. The *Online Optimized PQ* [12] applied optimized PQ to dynamic data. To this end, they solve SVD to optimize the rotation matrix when a new vector is added. As we can see, it is expensive to solve SVD against high-dimensional data.

3   Related Work

This section reviews the related work around the approximate nearest-neighbor search and product quantization.

3.1   Approximate Nearest-Neighbor (ANN) Search

Approximate nearest-neighbor (ANN) search methods are useful in many real applications when we do not need completely accurate results while we need to save computational and memory costs. There is a trade-off between accuracy and costs in time/space, and we need to choose the appropriate method by taking into account such characteristics.

Typically, we can categorize ANN methods according to the way that they transform the data (vectors) and the data structure to store the data. Table 1 summarizes the characteristics of the three types of methods.

Table 1. Characteristics of ANN Search

	Hash	Tree	Quantization
Accuracy	Low	High	Medium
Comp. cost	Low	High	Medium
Memory cost	Low	High	Medium

Hash-based methods, such as locally sensitive hashing (LSH) [4], use a hash function to map similar vectors to similar hash codes with high probability. By mapping to hash codes in this way, many vectors can be approximated by a small number of hash codes, thereby reducing the memory requirement. In addition, when computing the similarity (or distance) between vectors, we can approximate it by the Hamming distance between the hash code, which significantly reduces the computational cost compared to the naive computation.

On the other hand, since a large number of vectors are represented by a single hash code, the conversion error becomes large, and the accuracy of retrieval is significantly affected.

In the tree-based methods such as kd-tree [16], the vectors are stored in a tree structure according to their spatial proximity in the vector space in such a way that search spaces are localized. We traverse the tree by visiting subtrees close to the query vector when performing ANN queries. Thus we can reduce the number of vectors to investigate. In the meantime, the space cost and computational cost are still high because the original vectors are stored without any compression, and the distance calculation between vectors is performed against the original vectors.

Quantization-based methods, such as product quantization (PQ) [9], exploit vector quantization to compress vectors as one or more codewords. Unlike the hash-based method, we can use multiple codewords to represent a vector, resulting in reduced error. Therefore, they offer more accurate results in ANN queries. Besides, the distance calculation is much faster than the tree-based methods because we can make a lookup table for a given query. As a result, we can avoid expensive and massive distance calculations.

As can be observed, the quantization-based methods offer good trade-off between accuracy and efficiency in time and space compared to other approaches.

3.2 Quantization Methods

This section briefly reviews related works around the original product quantization [9]. Some of its extensions exploit pretransformation to the vectors [7,14]. Specifically, they apply a rotation matrix against the vectors to minimize the quantization error. As a result, they can also improve search accuracy.

Some methods exploit multiple codewords to represent multiple codebooks [2,17]. Thus, they can improve the search accuracy by representing a subvector as a set of codewords from the codebooks.

Additive quantization [1] and composite quantization [21] attempt to generalize vector quantization so that it allows us to apply vector operations on compressed codewords without decompression. Besides, some methods use generalized pre-quantization algorithms for different objectives, such as to improve encoding speed [22], to use training data [18], to use multimodal models [23]. [12,20] try to apply online learning to the codebooks to deal with stream data. None of the existing methods has tried to apply online PQ to dynamic data.

4   Proposed Method

As we observed, optimized PQ presents a good performance than ordinary PQ, while it requires expensive SVD to optimize rotation matrix. To adapt it to dynamic data, we proposed to apply SVD-Updating that allow us to solve SVD against dynamic data in an efficient way. Basically, we employ the approach proposed in Online PQ [20] and extend it by introducing rotation to reduce the quantization error, where the codebooks and the rotation matrix are alternatively optimized. In the following, we describe the details of the proposed method.

4.1   Updating Codebook

First, we describe the process of updating the codebook. The algorithm used in Online PQ is used to update the codebook. Extending the objective function described in the Eq. 7, we obtain Eq. 8.

$$\min_{R, C^{t,1} \cdots C^{t,M}} \sum_{X} \sum_{m=1}^{M} \| x^{t,m} - c_i^{t,m}(x^{t,m}) \|^2,$$

$$s.t. C^t = \{ R^t c^t \in C^t = C^{t,1} \times \cdots \times C^{t,M} \} \tag{8}$$

where C is the codebook and R is the rotation matrix. An extension of the optimization of this objective function using a rotation matrix [20] is shown in Eq. 9.

$$c_k^{t+1,m} = c_k^{t,m} + \frac{1}{n_k^m} (\hat{x}^{t,m} - c_k^{t,m}) \tag{9}$$

where $x^{t,m}$ is the m-th subvector of the input vector at time t, $c_k^{t,m}$ is the codeword corresponding to $x_k^{t,m}$, and n_k^m is the number of vectors in the cluster to which the codeword $c_k^{t,m}$ belongs $\hat{x}_k^{t+1,m} = x^{t,m} R^t$. The rotation matrix R^t at time t, which has already been computed, is used for the pre-transformation. Although a pre-transformation is calculated, the computation of the update process is the same as for Online PQ. Intuitively, this computation can be understood as an operation to modify the position of the corresponding cluster center. The computation repositions each codeword so that the cluster centroid is located at the center of gravity of the cluster containing the new vector. Updating codebook can be computed using only the new vector x. Therefore, the computational complexity is independent of the size of the existing dataset already entered into the database.

4.2   Update Rotation Matrix using SVD-Updating

As well as codebooks, when new vectors are added, the existing rotation matrix is not optimal for the data with the new data. The optimal rotation matrix can be obtained by solving the orthogonal Procrustes problem [15], which can be solved by SVD. Suppose that the optimal rotation matrix is obtained as in Eq. 10 where X is the input vector and Y is the vector generated from the codebook.

$$SVD(XY^T) = USV^T$$
$$R = VU^T \tag{10}$$

In this work we employ SVD-Updating [3] to solve the problem without decomposing whole matrix. Besides, it allows us to approximate the vectors by low-rank singular value decomposition, thereby saving the computation. The original SVD-Updating was proposed to address the problem of recommender systems where the matrix represent user-item relationship. In the following, we show how we can adapt it to optimize the rotation matrix in OPQ.

When a new vector X' is added, we want to solve the following formula without recalculating the entire matrix.

$$W = A_k + X'Y'^T \tag{11}$$

$$SVD(W) = U_W S_W V_W{}^T \tag{12}$$

$$R_W = V_W U_W{}^T \tag{13}$$

where A_k is obtained by a low-rank approximation of $A = XY^T$,

$$SVD(A) \approx SVD(A_k) = U_k S_k V_k^T \tag{14}$$

From Eqs. 11 and 14, we get:

$$W = U_k S_k V_k^T + X'Y'^T \tag{15}$$

$$\therefore U_k^T W V_k = S_k + U_k^T X'Y'^T V_k \tag{16}$$

Then,

$$Q = S_k + U_k^T X'Y'^T V_k \tag{17}$$

$$SVD(Q) = U_Q S_Q V_Q^T \tag{18}$$

From Eq. 12, 16 and 17, we get:

$$U_k^T U_W S_W V_W^T V_k = U_Q S_Q V_Q^T \tag{19}$$

$$\therefore U_W = U_k U_Q \tag{20}$$

$$\therefore S_W = S_k \tag{21}$$

$$\therefore V_W = V_k V_Q \tag{22}$$

In this way, the U_W, S_W and V_W can be obtain by Eq. 20, 21 and 22. Thus, the new rotation matrix R_W is calculated as follows:

$$R_W = V_W U_W^T$$
$$= V_k V_Q U_Q^T U_k^T \tag{23}$$

$$(Q = S_k + U_k^T X'Y'^T V_k, SVD(Q) = U_Q S_Q V_Q^T)$$

In other words, the new rotation matrix R_W in Eq. 15 only needs to compute SVD of the $(k \times k)$ matrix Q, instead of computing the SVD of $(r \times r)$ matrix W in Eq. 11.

4.3   Online Optimized PQ Using SVD-Updating

The overall algorithm of the proposed online OPQ with SVD-Updating is shown in Algorithm 1.

Algorithm 1. Online Optimized PQ

Input: $\{x \in \mathbb{R}^{N \times D}\}$ //Streaming datasets
   R //Rotation matrix
   value of low rank approximation l
   initialize $M \times K$ sub-codebook $c_{1,1}^0, \cdots, c_{m,k}^0, \cdots, c_{M,K}^0$ by OPQ
   initialize $M \times K$ counters $n_{1,1}^0, \cdots, n_{m,k}^0, \cdots, n_{M,K}^0$ that indicate the number of initial data assigned to the $c_{m,k}^0$
Output: R^t //Rotation matrix
1: $[U_l^0, S_l^0, V_l^0] \leftarrow \text{LowRankApproximation}(U, S, V, l)$
2: for $t \leftarrow 1$ to N do
3:    $\hat{x}^t \leftarrow x^t R$
4:    //(i) update the codebook
5:    $[c^{t+1}, n^{t+1}] \leftarrow \text{updateCodebook}(c^t, \hat{x}^t, n^t)$
6:    //(ii)update the Rotation matrix
7:    $Q^t \leftarrow S_l^t + U_l^{t^T} \cdot x^t \cdot c^t(x^t) \cdot V_l^t$
8:    $[U_Q, S_Q, V_Q] \leftarrow \text{SVD}(Q^t)$
9:    $U_l^{t+1} \leftarrow U_l^t U_Q$
10:   $S_l^{t+1} \leftarrow S_Q$
11:   $V_l^{t+1} \leftarrow V_l^t V_Q$
12:   $R^{t+1} \leftarrow V_l^{t+1} U_l^{t+1^T}$

4.4   Computational Complexity

Time Complexity. The transformation of the input vector x by the rotation matrix R takes $\mathcal{O}(ND^2)$. To update the codebook, online PQ requires $\mathcal{O}(NDK + NM + ND)$. Next, updating the rotation matrix requires $\mathcal{O}(ND^2l^2)$ for the calculation of matrix Q, SVD on the $(l \times l)$ matrix requires $\mathcal{O}(l^3)$, and $\mathcal{O}(Dl^2)$ is neede for calculating $U^{(t+1)_l}$ and $V^{(t+1)_l}$. Finally, the computation of the updated rotation matrix R^{t+1} is $\mathcal{O}(D^2l)$. From the above, the time calculation complexity of the whole algorithm is R^{t+1} is $\mathcal{O}(DK + NM + ND^2l^2 + l^3 + Dl^2 + D^2l)$.

Space Complexity. The rotation matrix R requires $\mathcal{O}(D^2)$, the codebook requires $\mathcal{O}(KD)$, and the counter $n_{m,k}^0$, which counts the number of data belonging to each codeword for updating the codebook requires $\mathcal{O}(KM)$. The spatial computation of the matrices Q, U_l^t, S_l^t and V_l^t required to update the rotation matrix is $\mathcal{O}(l^2), \mathcal{O}(Dl), \mathcal{O}(l^2), \mathcal{O}(Dl)$ respectively. From the above, the spatial computation of the whole algorithmis $\mathcal{O}(D^2 + KD + KM + 2Dl + 2l^2)$.

4.5 Applying Sliding Window

As we have discussed, the proposed method allows us to efficiently update the codebooks and the rotation matrix according to the new incoming data. Note here that, in many applications, users tend to be more interested in recent data than old data. In such cases, it might not be suitable to keep all past data in a dynamic database because it might affect the search accuracy. Instead, we can remove old data as new data come in the database.

Online PQ addresses this problem by employing a *sliding window* instead of batch-based updating. A sliding window moves by the fixed shift size as new data arrives, and the data getting out of the window are removed. This makes it possible to gradually update the currently available data set according to the latest trends in the updates against the database.

Now, we discuss how to adapt the proposed scheme to the window-based model. The actual calculation is shown in the following Eq. 24.

$$\hat{c}_k^{t+1,m} = c_k^{t,m} - \frac{1}{n_k^m}(\hat{x}^{t,m} - c_k^{t,m}) \tag{24}$$

Equation 24 is simply the inversion of the sign of the equation. This calculation uses the data removed from the window to update the position of the codeword. As a result, This calculation removes the effect of the old data on the codebook.

Next, we show how to update the rotation matrix. It is similar to the approach for updating the codebook. Let $\hat{X}$ be the vector removed from the window and $\hat{Y}$ be the vector regenerated from the codebook.

$$\hat{W} = A_k - \hat{X}'\hat{Y}'^T \tag{25}$$

$$SVD(\hat{W}) = U_{\hat{W}} S_{\hat{W}} V_{\hat{W}}{}^T \tag{26}$$

$$R_{\hat{W}} = V_{\hat{W}} U_{\hat{W}}{}^T \tag{27}$$

$\hat{W}$ is the inverted sign of W in the Eq. 11. As in the case of the insertion update process, the calculation of the singular value decomposition by SVD-Updating here is calculated as follows:

$$\hat{Q} = S_k - U_k^T \hat{X}' \hat{Y}'^T V_k \tag{28}$$

$$SVD(\hat{Q}) = U_{\hat{Q}} S_{\hat{Q}} V_{\hat{Q}^T} \tag{29}$$

In the above equations, we can remove the effect of the old data from the rotation matrix without recalculating the entire matrix.

5 Experiments

5.1 Experimental Setting

To evaluate the performance of the proposed method, we have conducted a set of experiments. The comparative methods are PQ, optimized PQ, online PQ, and online OPQ. Besides, we tested the case where the model (codebook and rotation matrix) is trained only once in the beginning as the baseline (labeled as "no update"). On the other hand, we tried the best case where the model is retrained with the entire dataset whenever a new batch is added (labeled as "all"). For online PQ, we updated the codebook only with the latest batch. For online OPQ, there are two cases:1) updates the codebook and rotation matrix with the conventional algorithm which is without SVD-Updating (labeled as "online opq") and 2) the proposed method which is using SVD-Updating (labeled as "online opq(SVD-updating)").

The comparison metrics are Recall@R and update time. Recall@R is the probability that the ground-truth nearest neighbor data is contained within the top R data extracted as approximate nearest neighbors. Update time is the running time required to update the codebook (and rotation matrix) in each model.

We experimented with three different datasets [6,11,19], including text and images. The details of datasets are shown in Table 2. Each dataset is queried with an input batch, and then the model is updated with it. For the text data, the dataset is ordered in chronological order. For image datasets, they are divided into classes (comprising two batches for one class) according to the class label to simulate the change in data distribution over time.

Table 2. dataset

Dataset	#Classes	Size	Feature	#Dim
News20 [11]	20	18,846	BERT	768
Caltech101 [6]	101	9,144	GIST	960
SUN397 [19]	397	108,753	GIST	960

5.2   Effects of Low-Rank Approximation

We tested the performance with different rank values. The experimental results are shown in Fig. 1. Each value represents the ratio of the approximated rank to the original dimensionality (e.g., 0.8 for 960-dimension means 768-dimension). Besides, we checked the rank of the matrix of the first batch (labeled as "auto") and used the value to approximate the matrix (Table 3). In terms of update time, the lower rank cases performed better due to their reduced amount of computation.

In the meantime, for the recall values, there is no much difference between the full and low-rank results. This implies that it is possible for us to focus on meaningful dimensions (out of full dimensions) to perform an NN search so that we can maintain the recall while achieving faster computation over low-ranked matrices. In the subsequent experiments, we use "auto" as the low-rank approximation.

Table 3. Calculated rank value for each dataset

Dataset	Rank
News20	267
Caltech101	112
SUN397	77

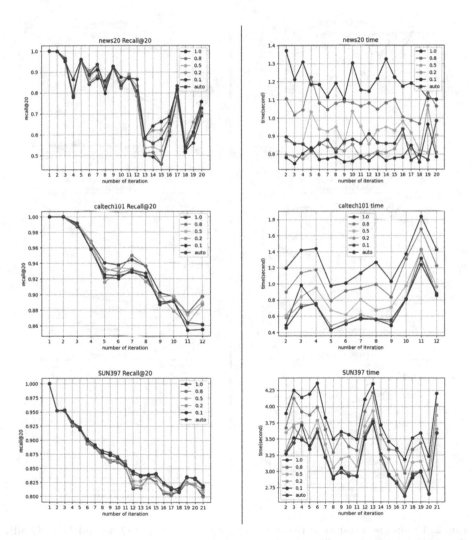

Fig. 1. Comparison results of Recall@20, update time with low rank approximation for each dataset

5.3   Comparison with Non-online Methods

The results of the comparison experiments with PQ and OPQ are shown in Fig. 2. Recall shows that the proposed method is better than the "no update" method. This is because the "no update" method trains the model in the first batch and does not update the model. As a result, it does not adapt to the newer batches. The "all" method retrains the model using all the data and thus shows a better recall than others, including the proposed method.

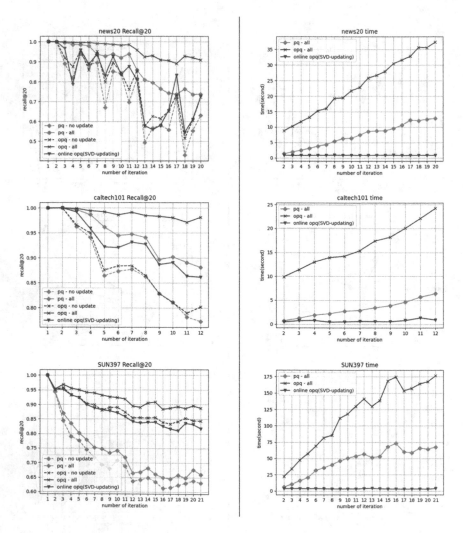

Fig. 2. Comparison results of Recall@20 and update time of PQ(no update), PQ(all), OPQ(no update), OPQ(all) and online OPQ(SVD-Updating) for each dataset

On the other hand, in comparing the update time, the "all" method increases as more batches are input. This is because training is performed on all batches, including the input batches, leading to a longer time for training with increasing data. The OPQ update time increases more than that of PQ because both the codebook and the rotation matrix need to be optimized. On the other hand, in the proposed method, the update time is constant. This is because it can update the model using only the input batch data (and not all data).

5.4   Comparison with Online Methods

We compared the performance among the online algorithms, i.e., online PQ, online OPQ, and online OPQ (SVD-Updating). The experimental results are shown in Fig. 3. We can observe that the degradation in recall for online OPQ is smaller than that of online PQ. The SUN397 dataset, which contains many data records, showed a significant difference in recall values. In the News20 and caltech101 datasets, the recall values of online OPQ and online OPQ (SVD-Updating) are almost the same, while online OPQ was slightly better than online OPQ (SVD-Updating) on the SUN397 dataset.

In terms of processing time, the proposed scheme was much faster than online OPQ - about 2x faster than online OPQ on the News20 dataset. This is because the size of the matrix to be computed for updating the rotation matrix is smaller because of the efficiency in low-rank approximation with SVD-Updating.

In summary, we can say that the proposed online OP with SVD-Updating achieved a good trade-off between recall and efficiency.

5.5   Performance with Sliding Windows

We show the experimental results of the method using sliding windows. We used the two datasets and applied the sliding window to update the codebooks, and the step size was fixed. Specifically, for the News20 dataset, the window width was set to 2,000 and the step size to 500. For the Caltech101 dataset, the window width was set to 1,000, and the step size was set to 100.

To compare the accuracy, we measured the Recall@20 values for each dataset, where the queries were generated by randomly choosing those data that were added to the window whenever the window slided. Figure 4 shows the results comparing the performance with sliding windows. We compared the proposed method (Online Optimized PQ using SVD-Updating) against the existing methods (Online PQ). The notation (deletion) indicates that the codebook and rotation matrix were updated using data removed from the window. The News20 dataset shows the best values for several iterations. This is because the data distribution used in the query is dominated by data that follows the new data distribution.

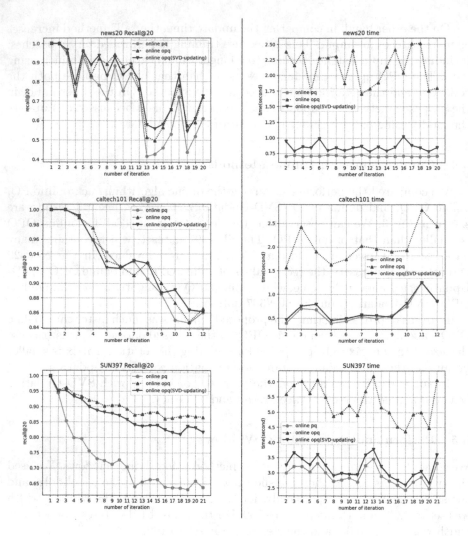

Fig. 3. Comparison results of Recall@20 and update time of online PQ, online OPQ and online OPQ(SVD-Updating) for each dataset

On the other hand, the Caltech101 dataset did not perform well as expected. This is probably due to the data's characteristics that the distribution does not change significantly, and thus removing old data form the window gave a negative impact to the performance.

As a result, we can observe that the sliding window method works well only if the parameters (e.g., window size and slide size) are configured according to the nature of the dataset and the requirements of the user as well.

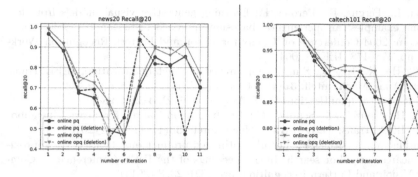

Fig. 4. Comparison results of Recall@20 with sliding window methods

6 Conclusion

In this paper we have proposed an efficient method for approximate NN search over dynamic data based on online OPQ, where the rotation matrix can be updated efficiently using SVD-Updating. It allows us to update the model without conducting SVD over the entire dataset. The experimental results have shown that the proposed method outperformed the previous studies and achieved a better trade-off between recall and efficiency.

Our future research includes further improve the performance by employing more sophisticated methods, such as Locally Optimized PQ [10].

Acknowledgments. This paper was supported by Japan Society for the Promotion of Science (JSPS) KAKENHI under Grant Number JP22H03694 and the New Energy and Industrial Technology Development Organization (NEDO) Grant Number JPNP20006.

References

1. Babenko, A., Lempitsky, V.: Additive quantization for extreme vector compression. In: Proceedings of the IEEE Conference on Computer Vision and Pattern Recognition, pp. 931–938 (2014)
2. Babenko, A., Lempitsky, V.: Tree quantization for large-scale similarity search and classification. In: Proceedings of the IEEE Conference on Computer Vision and Pattern Recognition, pp. 4240–4248 (2015)
3. Berry, M.W., Dumais, S.T., O'Brien, G.W.: Using linear algebra for intelligent information retrieval. SIAM Rev. **37**(4), 573–595 (1995)
4. Datar, M., Immorlica, N., Indyk, P., Mirrokni, V.S.: Locality-sensitive hashing scheme based on p-stable distributions. In: Proceedings of the Twentieth Annual Symposium on Computational Geometry, pp. 253–262 (2004)
5. Dong, A., Bhanu, B.: Concept learning and transplantation for dynamic image databases. In: Proceedings of 2003 International Conference on Multimedia and Expo, ICME 2003, (Cat. No. 03TH8698), vol. 1, pp. I-765. IEEE (2003)

6. Fei-Fei, L., Fergus, R., Perona, P.: Learning generative visual models from few training examples: an incremental bayesian approach tested on 101 object categories. In: 2004 Conference on Computer Vision and Pattern Recognition Workshop, pp. 178–178. IEEE (2004)
7. Ge, T., He, K., Ke, Q., Sun, J.: Optimized product quantization. IEEE Trans. Pattern Anal. Mach. intell. **36**(4), 744–755 (2013)
8. Gray, R.: Vector quantization. IEEE Assp Mag. **1**(2), 4–29 (1984)
9. Jegou, H., Douze, M., Schmid, C.: Product quantization for nearest neighbor search. IEEE Trans. Pattern Anal. Mach. Intell. **33**(1), 117–128 (2010)
10. Kalantidis, Y., Avrithis, Y.: Locally optimized product quantization for approximate nearest neighbor search. In: Proceedings of the IEEE Conference on Computer Vision and Pattern Recognition, pp. 2321–2328 (2014)
11. Lang, K.: Newsweeder: learning to filter netnews. In: Machine Learning Proceedings 1995, pp. 331–339. Elsevier (1995)
12. Liu, C., Lian, D., Nie, M., Xia, H.: Online optimized product quantization. In: 2020 IEEE International Conference on Data Mining (ICDM), pp. 362–371. IEEE (2020)
13. Moffat, A., Zobel, J., Sharman, N.: Text compression for dynamic document databases. IEEE Trans. Knowl. Data Eng. **9**(2), 302–313 (1997)
14. Norouzi, M., Fleet, D.J.: Cartesian k-means. In: Proceedings of the IEEE Conference on computer Vision and Pattern Recognition, pp. 3017–3024 (2013)
15. Schönemann, P.H.: A generalized solution of the orthogonal procrustes problem. Psychometrika **31**(1), 1–10 (1966)
16. Silpa-Anan, C., Hartley, R.: Optimised kd-trees for fast image descriptor matching. In: 2008 IEEE Conference on Computer Vision and Pattern Recognition, pp. 1–8. IEEE (2008)
17. Wang, J., Wang, J., Song, J., Xu, X.S., Shen, H.T., Li, S.: Optimized cartesian k-means. IEEE Trans. Knowl. Data Eng. **27**(1), 180–192 (2014)
18. Wang, X., Zhang, T., Qi, G.J., Tang, J., Wang, J.: Supervised quantization for similarity search. In: Proceedings of the IEEE Conference on Computer Vision and Pattern Recognition, pp. 2018–2026 (2016)
19. Xiao, J., Hays, J., Ehinger, K.A., Oliva, A., Torralba, A.: Sun database: large-scale scene recognition from abbey to zoo. In: 2010 IEEE Computer Society Conference on Computer Vision and Pattern Recognition, pp. 3485–3492. IEEE (2010)
20. Xu, D., Tsang, I.W., Zhang, Y.: Online product quantization. IEEE Trans. Knowl. Data Eng. **30**(11), 2185–2198 (2018)
21. Zhang, T., Du, C., Wang, J.: Composite quantization for approximate nearest neighbor search. In: International Conference on Machine Learning, pp. 838–846. PMLR (2014)
22. Zhang, T., Qi, G.J., Tang, J., Wang, J.: Sparse composite quantization. In: Proceedings of the IEEE Conference on Computer Vision and Pattern Recognition, pp. 4548–4556 (2015)
23. Zhang, T., Wang, J.: Collaborative quantization for cross-modal similarity search. In: Proceedings of the IEEE Conference on Computer Vision and Pattern Recognition, pp. 2036–2045 (2016)

Empirical Study of the Model Generalization for Argument Mining in Cross-Domain and Cross-Topic Settings

Alaa Alhamzeh[1,2(✉)], Előd Egyed-Zsigmond[1], Dorra El Mekki[2],
Abderrazzak El Khayari[2], Jelena Mitrović[2,3], Lionel Brunie[1],
and Harald Kosch[2]

[1] INSA de Lyon, 20 Avenue Albert Einstein, 69100 Villeurbanne, France
{Elod.Egyed-zsigmond,Lionel.Brunie}@insa-lyon.fr
[2] Universität Passau, Innstraße 41, 94032 Passau, Germany
{Alaa.Alhamzeh,Jelena.Mitrovic,Harald.Kosch}@uni-passau.de,
{elmekk01,elkhay01}@ads.uni-passau.de
[3] Institute for AI Research and Development, Fruškogorska 1, 21000 Novi Sad, Serbia

Abstract. To date, the number of studies that address the generalization of argument models is still relatively small. In this study, we extend our stacking model from argument identification to an argument unit classification task. Using this model, and for each of the learned tasks, we address three real-world scenarios concerning the model robustness over multiple datasets, different domains and topics. Consequently, we first compare single-dataset learning (SDL) with multi-dataset learning (MDL). Second, we examine the model generalization over completely unseen dataset in our cross-domain experiments. Third, we study the effect of sample and topic sizes on the model performance in our cross-topic experiments. We conclude that, in most cases, the ensemble learning stacking approach is more stable over the generalization tests than a transfer learning DistilBERT model. In addition, the argument identification task seems to be easier to generalize across shifted domains than argument unit classification. This work aims at filling the gap between computational argumentation and applied machine learning with regard to the model generalization.

Keywords: Argument mining · Robustness · Generalization ·
Multi-dataset learning · Cross-domain · Cross-topic

1 Introduction

Human communication is a complex function of language, facial expressions, tone of speech, and body language. We communicate to express our feelings, opinions, and beliefs which are a result of many arguments we believe in. Those

© Springer-Verlag GmbH Germany, part of Springer Nature 2022
A. Hameurlain and A. M. Tjoa (Eds.): *Transactions on Large-Scale Data- and Knowledge-Centered Systems LII*, LNCS 13470, pp. 103–126, 2022.
https://doi.org/10.1007/978-3-662-66146-8_5

arguments may have been influenced by a life experience, a known fact, analogies or something else. However, to persuade the other party by our point of view, we have to present and explain those different arguments to them. Argumentation, therefore, has been remarked and studied since the 6th century B.C. by Ancient Greek philosophers. Aristotle's Logic [1], and in particular his Theory of the syllogism has laid the groundwork for the definitions of logical reasoning and arguments of today.

Given this historical dimension of argumentation studies, there has been a large number of different argumentation theories which align with different aspects of argumentation [2]. The same applies to the argument quality criteria. Similarly, there have been numerous proposals for assessing the merits or defects of an argument.

The argument, in its simplest form, consists of one claim (also called a conclusion [3]) supported by at least one premise [4]. The premise, which is also known as the evidence, is the reason or justification for the connected claim. Figure 1 shows an example of an argumentative student essay [5] regarding the controversial topic "having children and quality of life". In this example, the argument units 1, 2, and 3 are premises related to the claim marked in argument unit 4. Moreover, we see in this example an instance for a "Support" relation between premise 1, premise 3 and the final claim as well as to an "Attack" relation between the premise 2 and the final claim. We have to note at this point, that an attack relation does not necessarily imply a bad or invalid argument. Indeed, discussing a potential rebuttal is a common strategy to prevent any potential criticism. In other words, the author states the contrary opinion (argument unit 2) and then states why it is not relevant (argument unit 3) which makes the overall argument stronger and more likely to be convincing.

"[Raising your own child is like having an important goal in your live]$_1$. Admittedly, [you will have great responsibilities and you also will have sleepiness nights]$_2$ but [these drawbacks will turn into a valuable experience when your kids become older]$_3$. Therefore, [Having children is the ultimate bliss in our lives]$_4$."

Fig. 1. Example of arguments (as taken from Student Essays Corpus [5])

Argument mining (AM) has been a self-established field of natural language processing in the last decade. That can be justified by the wide spectrum of its practical applications. For instance, computer-assisted writing [6], fact checking [7], and decision support systems like the one presented in [3] for legal counselling and [8] for comparative question answering. That points out the value of argumentation in interdisciplinary settings.

However, generalizing over different domains is still one of the hardest challenges in computational argumentation. Moreover, there is still a research space for improving the assessment of model stability from machine learning point of view. The model robustness is its performance stability over new variants comparing to the training stage. Mainly, robustness over new data distribution (e.g., [9]) or different model runs (e.g., [10]). We examine both aspects in our experiments. Therefore, we aim in this study, to extend our previous work [11], by performing a deep analysis on our stacked model from two perspectives:

- Machine learning perspective: we evaluate the robustness of our model in different cross-domain and cross-topic settings.
- Argument mining perspective: we perform a comprehensive feature analysis on how "argumentativeness" is similarly (mis)captured across diverse datasets.

To this end, we also integrate a third corpus and apply multiple methodologies for two argumentation classification tasks. Consequently, the contributions of this study are:

1. First, we move a step towards another argumentation task which is argument unit classification task (premise/claim classification). We investigate that using the same two primarily used corpora, with a new integrated dataset from the IBM Project Debater[1]. We, henceforth, apply all of our experiments, for both learned tasks: argument identification and argument unit classification.
2. We start by a preliminary step with respect to the model selection on our stacked approach, and we report on the best combination of features to be adopted in our further experiments.
3. We examine if including more data during the training stage (Multi-dataset learning), would increase the performance reported using one dataset (Single-dataset learning).
4. Moreover, to assess the model generalization ability and robustness over shifted data distributions, we set up a cross-domain experiment where we test the model on a completely unseen corpus.
5. Similarly, we apply cross-topic experiments, where, in each run, a unique set of unseen topics is saved apart for testing. In addition, this experiment aims at examining how the number of training topics influences the model generalization performance over unseen topics.
6. To foster the work in this area, our source-code is available publicly through our github repository[2]

This paper is organized as follows: in Sect. 2, we take a close look at the conceptual background of our work as well as the literature studies considering our points of interest. In Sect. 3, we present the problem statement as well as an overview on the data, and our stacked models that compose the cornerstone of the experiments examined in this paper. We employ a deep feature analysis and model selection and we examine the generalization of the selected model on various cross scenarios in Sect. 4. Finally, we discuss the overall research questions and future work in Sect. 5.

---

[1] https://research.ibm.com/interactive/project-debater/index.html.
[2] https://github.com/Alaa-Ah/Stacked-Model-for-Argument-Mining.

2   Related Work

The basic challenge of the AM research field is its variance over domains and topics. The model falls short in shifted domain settings. Therefore, the search for a domain-agnostic model was a point of interest for many researches. One of the proposed solutions towards this, is to use transfer learning models. Liga et al. [12] aimed at discriminating evidence related to argumentation schemes. They used three different pre-trained transformers to generate multiple sentence embeddings, then trained classifiers on it. Wambsganss et al. [13] proposed an approach for argument identification using BERT on multiple datasets. Our stacked model overcomes theirs on the Student Essays corpus achieving an accuracy of 91.62% and F1-score of 84.83% compared to their accuracy of 80.00% and F1-score of 85.19%. On the Web Discourse corpus, we have similar accuracy values (78.5% to 80.00%) while, on the level of the combined model, our approach achieved better performance even though they have investigated on more training corpora.

Besides transformers, adversarial learning has also been selected to test the model robustness over shifted data distribution by providing deceptive input. Indeed, the assumption behind adversarial learning in NLP, is that by generating variant samples across several domains, deep networks are resistant not only to heterogeneous texts but also to linguistic bias and noise [14]. Tzeng et al. proposed in [15] a novel unsupervised domain adaptation framework to identify transferable features that are suitable for two different domains. This approach showed promising results in unsupervised tasks.

Over time, cross-domain AM became a must. However, it has been mainly studied in a multi-dataset manner (or as multi-dataset learning (MDL) as addressed by [16]). For example, in the work of Ajjour et al. [17], they extend the argument unit segmentation task to investigate the robustness of the model while testing on three different corpora; the essays corpus [5], the editorials corpus [18], and the web discourse corpus [19]. Their proposed argument unit segmentation system is based on a neural network model incorporating features on a word-level setting on the in-domain level as well as cross-domain level. Their results show that structural and semantic features are the most effective in segmenting argument units across domains, whereas semantic features are best at identifying the boundaries of argumentative units within one domain. However, in their study, features are extracted at the token level whereas in our approach, we tackle the sentence level classification for our experiments within and across domains and for both argumentative sentence detection and argument component classification tasks.

In addition, [20] proposed the ArguWeb, a cross-domain argument mining CNN-based framework designed to first extract the argument from the web then segment it and classify its units. This approach tackles the two subtasks of argument mining: argument detection and argument component classification on both in-domain and cross-domain scenarios. In terms of cross-domain, the model was trained on two corpora and tested each time on a third one. The evaluation of the model's performance was conducted using character-level CNN, word-based CNN, SVM, and Naive Bayes in two scenarios: in-domain and cross-domain.

The results show that the character-level CNN outperforms other models when testing on web-extracted data such as the web-discourse corpus.

With respect to machine learning, we usually evaluate the prediction of models on an unseen split of the dataset and use that to report the performance of the model. Yet, this generalization could be limited to data that follow the same distribution which the model has already been trained on. In other words, the model memorized it rather that generalized over it. This issue has been studied by [21] and they conclude that quantifying train/test overlap is crucial to assessing real world applicability of machine learning in NLP tasks, especially when the training data is not large enough such as in a shared task case. According to [22], the key issue is that the algorithm training error provides an optimistically biased estimation, especially when the number of training samples is small. Therefore, many methods have been suggested to prevent this deviation from the empirical measurements. [10] investigated whether the linguistic generalization behaviour of a given neural architecture is consistent across multiple instances (i.e., runs) of that architecture. They found that models that differ only in their initial weights and the order of training examples can vary substantially in out-of-distribution linguistic generalization. Therefore, we always consider the average of 5 different runs along all our paper experiments.

Another interesting approach to measure robustness of a model is by using compositional generalization, which combines different parts of the test samples. An example would be, in image classification, adding rain or snow effect or rotating images in order to see if a self-driving car still recognizes the stop sign. This out-of-distribution generalization is known as Domain Generalization, which aims to learn a model from one or several different but related domains (i.e., diverse training datasets) that will generalize well on unseen testing domains [23]. We adopt this definition in our cross-domain experiments. We also derive a similar strategy with respect to unseen topics from the same dataset in our cross-topic experiments.

We also want to point out that several research fields are closely related to domain generalization, including but not limited to: transfer learning, multi-task learning, ensemble learning and zero-shot learning [23]. In our models, we have combined ensemble learning using a stacking approach and transfer learning using DistilBERT.

However, before we extend upon the experiments, we apply deep feature analysis and model selection, motivated by the work of [24] to set up the best model configuration for each of the two addressed AM tasks, namely argument identification and argument unit classification. To this end, we used three different corpora which are highly investigated in AM studies.

3   Method

In this section, we present the problem statement, the used corpora, and an overview on our stacking model [11], which we will further use in all our experiments.

3.1 Problem Statement

The problem of argument mining is vast and can be seen as a set of several sub-tasks. In this paper, we consider two of them: argument identification and argument unit classification as discourse analysis problems. In our approach, we classify the text at sentence level since it is less common to have two parts of an argument in one sentence. For example, Stab et al. [25] reported, for Student Essays corpus, that only 8.2% of all sentences need to be split in order to identify argument components. Moreover, a sentence with two different argumentative components will still be valid (and considered as an argument) on the level of argument identification task. Therefore, the first step will be always to apply a sentence segmentation then a binary classification of each sentence with respect to the particular task. In addition to the argument mining tasks, we aim at answering the following questions:

(1) What is the minimal set of features that can capture arguments and their units over different datasets? (Sect. 4.1).
(2) Is it beneficial to include data from different argument models to increase accuracy? (Sect. 4.2).
(3) To what extent is our AM approach independent of domain and data diversity? To tackle this point, we run a cross-domain experiment where we test on a completely unseen corpus (Sect. 4.3), and cross-topic experiments where we test on unseen topics from the same corpus (Sect. 4.4).

3.2 Data Description

In our work, we use three publicly available corpora:

The **Student Essays corpus**: contains 402 Essays about various controversial topics. This data has been introduced by Stab et al. [5]. The annotation covers three argument components, namely, 'major claim', 'claim', and 'premise'. Moreover, it presents the support/attack relations between them. Hence, it was used in several argument mining tasks. The dataset also includes one file called 'prompts' which describes the question behind each essay. We consider this 'prompt' as the topic of the essay.

The **User-generated Web Discourse corpus** is a smaller dataset that contains 340 documents about 6 controversial topics in education such as mainstreaming and prayer in schools. The document may refer to an article, blog post, comment, or forum posts. In other words, this is a noisy, unrestricted, and less formalized dataset. The annotation has been done by [19] following Toulmin's model [4]. Thus, it covers the argument components: 'claim', 'premise', 'backing' and 'rebuttal'.

The **IBM corpus** [26] consists of 2683 manually annotated argument components derived from Wikipedia articles on 33 controversial topics. It contains 1392 labeled claims and 1291 labeled evidence for 350 distinct claims in 12 different topics. In other words, there are only 1291 evidences derived from only

Table 1. Class distributions for all used datasets

Dataset	#Premise	#Claim	#Non-arg	#Topics
StudentEssays	3510	1949	1358	372
WebDiscourse	830	195	411	6
IBM	1291	1392	0	33

12 topics, while there are 1042 claims unsupported by evidence derived from 21 different topics. This dataset does not include a "Non-argument" label so we could not use it for the argument identification task. Instead, we used it only for experiments on argument unit classification.

Table 1 shows the class distributions for the three datasets. Moreover, different samples of those datasets are expressed in Table 2. We can clearly observe that they do not share the same characteristic like the text length and organization. This makes it more challenging to design a model that generalizes well over them.

Table 2. Text examples from the different datasets

Student Essays	IBM article	Web Discourse
"First of all, through cooperation, children can learn about interpersonal skills which are significant in the future life of all students. What we acquired from team work is not only how to achieve the same goal with others but more importantly, how to get along with others. On the other hand, the significance of competition is that how to become more excellence to gain the victory. Hence it is always said that competition makes the society more effective."	"Exposure to violent video games causes at least a temporary increase in aggression and this exposure correlates with aggression in the real world. The most recent large scale meta-analysis– examining *130 studies* with over *130,000 subjects* worldwide– concluded that exposure to violent video games causes both short term and long term aggression in players."	"I think it is a very loving thing, a good and decent thing to send children to a private school!"

3.3 Models of Our Ensemble Learning Approach

The main assumption behind ensemble learning is that when different models are correctly combined, the ensemble model tends to outperform each of the individual models in terms of accuracy and robustness [27]. We adopted this learning approach in our model in order to reach a trade-off between the pros and cons of classical and deep learning models. It is well known that the data scale drives deep learning progress, yet data labeling is an expensive and time-consuming process, especially given the nature of fine-grained hierarchical argumentation schemes as in the student essays corpus [24]. Whereas, in a small training set regime (which is usually the case in AM available datasets), a simple classical machine learning model may outperform a more complex neural network. In addition, training a classical model and interpreting it is much faster and easier than a neural network based one. On the other hand, traditional machine learning algorithms fall short as soon as the testing data distribution or the target task are not the same as the distribution of the training data and the learned task. In contrast, in transfer learning, the learning of new tasks relies on previously learned ones. The algorithm can store and access knowledge over different corpora and different tasks. Hence, we studied both directions of the learning algorithms and composed our final model as follows:

Classical Machine Learning Model - SVM
In terms of the first base model, we defined a set of diverse features inspired by the works of [24, 28]. We organize those features in sets of structural, lexical, and syntactic features in addition to discourse markers. Table 3 shows a complete list of each group of features as well as their description (more details about the reasoning behind each one can be found in our previous work [11]).

Transfer Learning Model (DistilBERT- Based)
 Transfer learning aims to apply previous learned knowledge from one source task (or domain) to a different target one, considering that source and target tasks and domains may be the same or may be different but share some similarities. Recently, BERT-like models got a lot of attention since they achieve state of the art results in different NLP tasks.

DistilBert [30] is trained on the same corpus like BERT [31] which consists of 16GB data (approximately 3.3 Billion words) from books corpus and Wikipedia. This large corpus of diverse topics enables it to show robust performance for domain-shift problems [32]. Figure 2 describes the adopted pipeline to perform the text classification using DistilBERT. The first block is the Tokenizer that takes care of all the BERT input requirements. The second block is the DistilBERT fine-tuned model, that outputs mainly a vector of length of 768 (default length). Our mission now is to adapt the output of this pre-trained model to our specific task. We achieve this by adding a third block, which is a linear layer applied on top of the DistilBERT transformer, and outputs a vector of size 2. The index of the maximum value in this vector represents the predicted class id. We trained the model for 3 epochs, using AdamW [33] as an optimizer and cross entropy for the loss calculation.

Table 3. Textual features. Our original added features are marked with '*'

Group	Feature	Description
Structural	sentence position [29]	Indicates the index of the sentence in the document.
	tokens count [28,29]	Indicates the count of tokens (words) in the sentence.
	question mark ending [29]	Boolean feature.
	punctuation marks count [29]	Indicates the number of punctuation marks in the sentence.
Lexical	1-3 g bow [28,29]	Unigrams, bigrams and trigram BoW features.
	1-2 g POS *	Unigram and bigram of POS features.
	NER *	count of the present named entities in the sentence.
Syntactic	parse tree depth [28,29]	Indicates the depth of the sentence's parse tree.
	sub-clauses count [28,29]	Indicates how many sub-clauses are in the sentence.
	verbal features *	counts of [modal, present, past, base form] verbs in the sentence
Discourse markers	keywords count [28,29]	Number of existing argument indicators ('actually','because', etc.).
	numbers count *	Indicates how many numbers in the sentence

Fig. 2. Transfer learning model architecture using DistilBERT

Ensemble Learning - Stacking (SVM + DistilBERT)

At this step, we have two heterogeneous based learners. One is based on textual features while the other is based on the NLP transformer's ability of language understanding. Therefore, a stacking approach fits perfectly to combine their predictions. As shown in Fig. 3, the outputs of SVM and DistilBert are used as input to the meta model that will learn how to produce the final prediction of a sentence based on the outputs of the base models. In order to have an array of independent features for the meta-model, and since SVM produces two probabilities $x'1$ and $x'2$ (i.e. $x'1 + x'2 = 1$), we consider only $x'1$. Whereas, $x1$ and $x2$ are two independent raw logits so both of them are considered. Given that we are dealing with a binary classification problem where the input features are independent, logistic regression serves well as a meta-model to accomplish the task. For the training/testing steps, we split first the combined dataset into 75% training and 25% for the overall testing. This testing data remains unseen

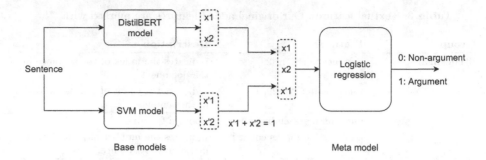

Fig. 3. Stacked model architecture for argument identification task

for all the models and it is used only for the final validation of the overall model. The base models are trained on the 75% training data. The training data of the meta model is prepared by 5-folds cross validation of the two base models. In each fold, the out-of-fold predictions are used as a part of the training data for the meta-model.

4   Experiments

In this section, we first take a preliminary stage to perform a model selection on our stacking method in Sect. 4.1. With the best found configurations, we move to our contribution regarding the examination of the model robustness and domain generalization in Sects. 4.2, 4.3 and 4.4. In all of our experiments, we address both argument identification and argument unit classification tasks.

4.1   Feature Analysis and Model Selection

We revisited our feature engineering part to assure the impact of each feature on its own and in correlation (or dependency) with other features. Including more features in the training can be problematic since it can increase space and computational time complexity. It can also introduce some noise according to unexpected value changes. These shortcomings are known as the curse of dimensionality. The main solution for dimensionality reduction is feature selection where different methods can be applied. In our work, we have first applied a *filter method* that is based on variance threshold such that we can figure out any features that do not vary widely between the three classes. We achieve that by visualizing the distribution's histogram of each feature. This helps us to see if a feature is important and improves the performance or if it has a redundant effect (or even no effect) on the final output. We present two examples in the following:

Figure 4 suggests that sentence position in the input paragraph correlates positively with premise sentences. In particular, with the positions 1 to 5. This means that a sentence that is stated earlier in the paragraph is more likely to be a premise than a claim or non-argument. We can see also that the value of position zero is very frequent since in WD and IBM, we do not have long paragraphs like in SE, rather it may be only one sentence.

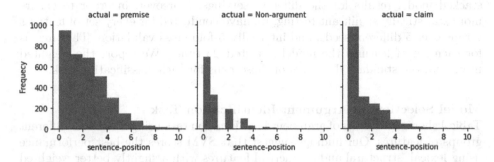

Fig. 4. Histograms of the *sentence position* feature

Similarly, Fig. 5 reflects the distribution of the punctuation marks over the three classes. We obviously can see that non-argument text tends to have more punctuation marks than argumentative text. Also, in terms of premise/claim classification, sentences with more than seven punctuation marks are only premises.

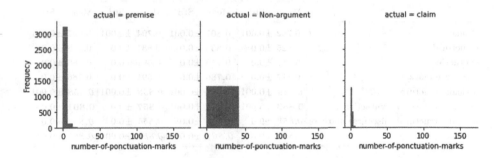

Fig. 5. Histograms of *number of punctuation marks* feature

Both "sentence position" and "number of punctuation marks" are part of our structural features which proved to be very essential in our model selection process. We identify the best performing model by conducting a *feature ablation tests*. Consequently, in order to determine the best configuration for our stacked model, we apply at this step a kind of a *wrapper method* that iterates through different combinations of features and performs a model retrain on each. For this model assessment, we adopt the accuracy as well as the weighted average metrics of precision, recall and F1-score since our data is imbalanced. The feature combination which results in the best model performance metrics for each AM task is selected.

Since the effect of different groups of features will be on the SVM performance in the first place, and subsequently on the stacking model that combines SVM with DistilBERT predictions, we report in this section, both SVM and stacked model results for the different settings. Moreover, in order to ensure more statistically significant testing, we have conducted for every set of features 5 runs over 5 different seeds, and internally 5-fold cross validation. That means for each set of features the model is tested 25 times. We report the weighted mean and the standard deviation of those runs for each classification task.

Model Selection on Argument Identification Task
Table 4 shows the results of argument identification task using SVM over different groups of features. Our findings suggest that SVM scores the best performance using lexical, structural and syntactical features with a slightly better weighted F1-score of 85.7% than SVM with all features or with lexical, structural and discourse markers (W-F1 score = 85.6%) while they all achieve the same accuracy of 86.1%

Table 4. Results of feature analysis on argument identification task using SVM on SE and WD

	W-Precision		W-Recall		W-F1 score		Accuracy	
	Mean	Std	Mean	Std	Mean	Std	Mean	Std
lexical	0.782	±0.001	0.807	±0.001	0.794	±0.001	0.807	±0.001
structural	0.825	±0.0	0.838	±0.0	0.831	±0.0	0.838	±0.0
syntactic	0.617	±0.0	0.786	±0.0	0.691	±0.0	0.786	±0.0
discourse markers	0.617	±0.0	0.786	±0.0	0.691	±0.0	0.786	±0.0
lexical, structural	*0.849*	*±0.001*	*0.858*	*±0.001*	*0.853*	*±0.001*	*0.858*	*±0.001*
lexical, structural, syntactical	**0.853**	*±0.001*	**0.861**	*±0.001*	**0.857**	*±0.0*	**0.861**	*±0.001*
lexical, structural, discourse markers	*0.852*	*±0.0*	*0.861*	*±0.0*	*0.856*	*±0.0*	*0.861*	*±0.0*
all features	*0.852*	*±0.0*	*0.861*	*±0.0*	*0.856*	*±0.001*	*0.861*	*±0.0*

Similarly, Table 5 confirms that the combination of structural, lexical and syntactical features achieves the best performance at the level of the stacked model. However, we observe that the scored mean of different settings is similar, especially when considering the structural features. According to the student-t test [34], when structural features are considered, the p-value exceeds 5%. Hence, we cannot claim that including (excluding) some features, except for structural and lexical, makes a huge difference on our model. Yet, we adopt the best performing model which empirically proved to be the model with structural, lexical and syntactical features for argument identification task. We, henceforth, use these settings for the upcoming experiments on this particular task.

Table 5. Results of model selection on argument identification using Stacked model on SE and WD

	W-Precision		W-Recall		W-F1 score		Accuracy	
	Mean	Std	Mean	Std	Mean	Std	Mean	Std
lexical	0.830	±0.004	0.842	±0.003	0.836	±0.003	0.842	±0.003
structural	0.851	±0.006	0.86	±0.005	0.856	±0.006	0.860	±0.005
syntactic	0.831	±0.006	0.843	±0.005	0.837	±0.006	0.843	±0.005
discourse markers	0.831	±0.007	0.843	±0.006	0.837	±0.007	0.843	±0.006
lexical, structural	*0.862*	±0.002	*0.869*	±0.002	*0.866*	+0.001	*0.869*	±0.002
lexical, structural, syntactical	**0.863**	±0.003	**0.870**	±0.003	**0.866**	±0.003	**0.870**	±0.003
lexical, structural, discourse markers	*0.861*	±0.004	*0.868*	±0.004	*0.865*	±0.004	*0.868*	±0.004
all features	*0.861*	±0.003	*0.868*	±0.002	*0.865*	±0.003	*0.868*	±0.002

Model Selection on Argument Unit Classification

To train the model on argument unit classification (i.e., premise/claim classification), we transform the feature "*Keywords count*" that indicates the count of any argument indicator, to two features: "*premise-indicators-count*" and "*claim-indicators-count*".

Furthermore, we also integrate a new dataset: IBM (cf. Table 1) and we further employ the model selection experiments as in the previous AM task. Table 6 confirms that SVM with all features delivers slightly better results compared to the other sub-combinations of features.

In terms of the stacked model, beside the semantic conceptual features that DistilBERT learns, we observe that the structural features are the most dominant proprieties that help to discriminate premises from claims in the three used corpora. However, they achieve a slight difference in comparison to their combination with lexical features and to the all features performance, as shown in Table 7. This finding is similar to the one by [17], which show that structural and semantic features are the most effective in segmenting argument units across domains.

Furthermore, Figs. 6 and 7 reports the F1 scores, and standard deviation, for SVM, DistilBERT and the stacked model across the different sets of features. We can observe that the stacked model scores at least the same performance of DistilBERT, and it improves over once the SVM classifier obtains a minimum score of 80% which is verified in most cases.

To sum up, in Sect. 4.1, we applied an in-depth feature analysis and model selection in two-folds: argument identification and argument unit classification. According to our findings, we ignore, henceforth, the features that lead to minor short-term wins, and we keep only the structural features for argument unit classification, and structural, lexical and syntactical features for argument identification task.

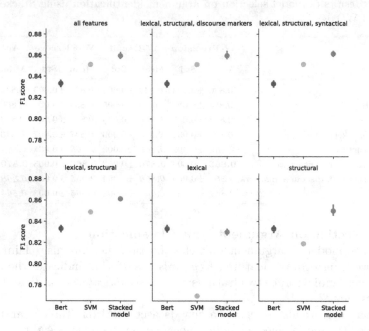

Fig. 6. Effect of feature selection on the argument identification task

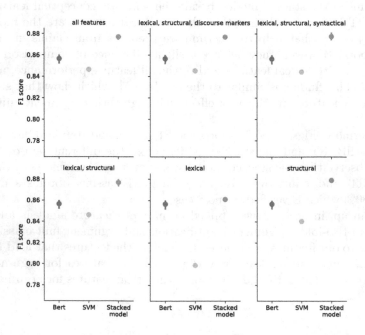

Fig. 7. Effect of feature selection on argument unit classification task

Table 6. Results of feature analysis on argument unit classification task using SVM on SE, WD and IBM datasets

	W-Precision		W-Recall		W-F1 score		Accuracy	
	Mean	Std	Mean	Std	Mean	Std	Mean	Std
lexical	0.802	±0.001	0.803	±0.001	0.802	±0.001	0.803	±0.001
structural	*0.840*	*±0.0*	*0.841*	*±0.0*	*0.841*	*±0.0*	*0.841*	*±0.0*
syntactic	0.378	±0.0	0.615	±0.0	0.468	±0.0	0.615	±0.0
discourse markers	0.633	±0.0	0.648	±0.0	0.640	±0.0	0.648	±0.0
lexical, structural	*0.847*	*±0.001*	*0.848*	*±0.001*	*0.847*	*±0.001*	*0.848*	*±0.001*
lexical, structural, syntactical	*0.846*	*±0.0*	*0.846*	*±0.0*	*0.846*	*±0.001*	*0.846*	*±0.0*
lexical, structural, discourse markers	*0.846*	*±0.0*	*0.847*	*±0.0*	*0.847*	*±0.001*	*0.847*	*±0.0*
all features	**0.848**	**±0.0**	**0.848**	**±0.0**	**0.848**	**±0.0**	**0.848**	**±0.0**

Table 7. Results of model selection on argument unit classification task using Stacked model on SE, WD, and IBM datasets

	W-Precision		W-Recall		W-F1 score		Accuracy	
	Mean	Std	Mean	Std	Mean	Std	Mean	Std
lexical	0.862	±0.002	0.863	±0.002	0.862	±0.002	0.863	±0.002
structural	**0.88**	**±0.002**	**0.88**	**±0.002**	**0.88**	**±0.002**	**0.88**	**±0.002**
syntactic	0.857	±0.003	0.857	±0.002	0.857	±0.002	0.857	±0.002
discourse markers	0.858	±0.003	0.858	±0.003	0.858	±0.002	0.858	±0.003
lexical, structural	*0.878*	*±0.003*	*0.878*	*±0.003*	*0.878*	*±0.003*	*0.878*	*±0.003*
lexical, structural, syntactical	*0.878*	*±0.004*	*0.879*	*±0.004*	*0.879*	*±0.004*	*0.879*	*±0.004*
lexical, structural, discourse markers	*0.878*	*±0.002*	*0.878*	*±0.002*	*0.878*	*±0.002*	*0.878*	*±0.002*
all features	*0.878*	*±0.002*	*0.878*	*±0.002*	*0.878*	*±0.003*	*0.878*	*±0.002*

4.2   Single-Dataset Learning (SDL) Vs. Multi-dataset Learning (MDL)

This experiment is intended to determine whether incorporating more datasets in the training step will generate a significant, positive impact on the robustness of the stacked model with respect to the test data, taking into account that our available datasets are relatively small. Consequently, we compare the outcomes of single-dataset learning and multi-dataset learning approaches.

In the SDL setup, we train and test the model on each dataset individually while in the MDL setup, we train the model on all datasets, but test on individual test split (20%) of the particular dataset. This methodology allows us to report performance scores on each dataset separately while training our model on a single versus multiple datasets.

We examine our model in these settings for the two trained tasks; argument identification and argument unit classification. However, since IBM has only the labels of argument components, we run the argument identification experiments

using WD and SE datasets, whereas we use WD, SE, and IBM for the argument
unit classification experiments. We use for each task its best stacked model
configuration conducted in Sect. 4.1.

Table 8. SDL vs. MDL argument identification using the stacked model.

		W-Precision		W-Recall		W-F1 score		Accuracy	
	Dataset	Mean	Std	Mean	Std	Mean	Std	Mean	Std
SDL	SE	**0.918**	±0.002	**0.92**	±0.002	**0.919**	±0.002	**0.92**	±0.002
	WD	**0.771**	±0.014	**0.776**	±0.011	**0.773**	±0.014	**0.776**	±0.011
MDL	SE	0.877	±0.006	0.881	±0.004	0.879	±0.004	0.881	±0.004
	WD	0.749	±0.011	0.765	±0.009	0.757	±0.015	0.765	±0.009

According to Table 8 and Table 9, we observe an expected drop in the performance for all datasets between the SDL and MDL setups. Yet, our stacked
model is still able, in all the cases, to produce reliable accuracy and F1-score.
Nevertheless, detecting argumentative text proved to be an intrinsically more
generalized task than determining the premises and claims. For example, the
variation of F1-score between the two settings, is in the range of $[-2\%, -4\%]$ for
argument identification, while it moves to the range of $[-7\%, -9\%]$ for argument
unit classification task.

These evaluation results also suggest that a single learning is always better
when we are sure that our future targeted data follows the same or a very close
distribution to the training one. This allows for better capturing of the dataset
characteristics. On the other hand, in a multi-dataset approach, merging the
datasets may introduce some noise if the model does not have enough samples
to weight the particular traits of the tested data.

4.3   Cross-Domain Settings: Testing on a Completely Unseen Dataset

The hypothesis behind the model generalization in machine learning, is its performance over the test split which stays unseen during the training process.
However, this assumption has a couple of caveats based on the fact that we are
drawing our test samples identically from the same distribution, and thus we
are not biasing ourselves in any way [23]. Hence, and in order to answer the
question: to which extent is our approach independent of the domain and data
diversity, we adopt another examination of the model robustness over shifted or
cross-domain settings. That is to say, we are testing on a completely new corpus
and not only a subset of unseen samples from the same training corpus. Consequently, this approach is also known as *out-of-domain* testing. However, it has

Table 9. SDL vs. MDL argument unit classification using the stacked model.

		W-Precision		W-Recall		W-F1 score		Accuracy	
	Dataset	Mean	Std	Mean	Std	Mean	Std	Mean	Std
SDL	SE	**0.825**	±0.003	**0.827**	±0.003	**0.826**	±0.003	**0.827**	±0.003
	WD	**0.888**	±0.012	**0.868**	±0.01	**0.878**	±0.007	**0.868**	±0.01
	IBM	**0.987**	±0.002	**0.987**	±0.002	**0.987**	±0.002	**0.987**	±0.002
MDL	SE	0.736	±0.134	0.738	±0.125	0.737	±0.127	0.738	±0.125
	WD	0.802	±0.026	0.796	±0.015	0.799	±0.014	0.796	±0.015
	IBM	0.913	±0.006	0.895	±0.008	0.904	±0.009	0.895	±0.008

been referred to as cross-domain in different argument mining studies (e.g., [9]). Therefore, we apply our experiments in a hold-out manner. In other words, we keep out in each run one dataset for testing and we train on the remaining ones. We again assay in these experiments our stacked model with only structural features for argument unit classification and with structural, lexical and syntactical features for argument identification task (cf. Sect. 4.1). We report the weighted mean and standard deviation over 5 different seeds.

The results of cross-domain argument identification and cross-domain argument unit classification are presented in Table 10 and Table 11 respectively.

Table 10. Evaluation of the cross-domain argument identification task.

			W-Precision		W-Recall		W-F1 score		Accuracy	
Training	Testing	Model	Mean	Std	Mean	Std	Mean	Std	Mean	Std
SE	WD	stacked model	0.559	±0.006	0.455	±0.013	0.502	±0.013	0.455	±0.013
		DistilBERT	**0.661**	±0.003	**0.694**	±0.003	**0.677**	±0.002	**0.694**	±0.003
		[9]					0.524		0.524	
WD	SE	stacked model	0.749	±0.006	0.771	±0.012	0.760	±0.006	0.771	±0.012
		DistilBERT	**0.759**	±0.006	**0.798**	±0.005	**0.778**	±0.004	**0.798**	±0.005
		[9]					0.128		0.181	

In terms of argument identification task, and based on the empirical evaluation presented in Table 10, we observe a satisfactory performance of our stacking model (W-F1 score= 0.76) when training on WD and testing on SE. However, the opposite scenario drastically reduces the performance where (W-F1 score= 0.502). While those are both better than the outcomes of [9] who used a binary statistical classifier with a similar set of our SVM features, DistilBERT is still able to outperform our stacking model in this scenario.

Table 11. Evaluation of the cross-domain argument unit classification task.

			W-Precision		W-Recall		W-F1 score		Accuracy	
Training	Testing	Model	Mean	Std	Mean	Std	Mean	Std	Mean	Std
SE, WD	IBM	stacked model	**0.766**	±0.015	**0.610**	±0.052	**0.679**	±0.081	**0.61**	±0.052
		DistilBERT	0.704	±0.028	0.550	±0.013	0.618	±0.024	0.55	±0.013
SE, IBM	WD	stacked model	0.735	±0.08	0.546	±0.281	0.627	±0.303	0.546	±0.281
		DistilBERT	**0.773**	±0.008	**0.805**	±0.009	**0.789**	±0.004	**0.805**	±0.009
WD,IBM	SE	stacked model	**0.677**	±0.013	**0.675**	±0.016	**0.676**	±0.044	**0.675**	±0.016
		DistilBERT	0.356	±0.128	0.586	±0.128	0.443	±0.141	0.586	±0.128

With regards to the argument unit classification (Table 11), we observe that training the stacked model on SE plus IBM and testing on WD yields worse results than training on other datasets (W-F1 score=0.627). However, it is still outperforming DistilBERT when testing on IBM and SE. In fact, the performance of DistilBERT degraded for this task, especially when testing on SE, and it achieves its best performance when testing on WD. That means, for premise/claim classification, we still need the features of SVM that allow our stacked model to overcome transfer learning once the tested corpus implies a formal structure that could be better learned using traditional machine learning. This also interprets the worst case of stacked model (trained on SE, IBM and tested on WD), since WD does not imply such learned features (e.g., sentence position) and by contrary SVM pulls back the stacked model performance in this testing scenario.

To sum up this section, our results suggest that transferring knowledge across different datasets is more applicable for argument identification task. Comparing to [11], DistilBERT is still reaching a higher accuracy when fine-tuned on the same dataset. This means that transfer learning is very efficient for in-domain-generalization, and less efficient for cross or out-of-domain generalization. However, this is even more challenging for argument unit classification where our stacking approach shows a better generalizing capability, in most cases, with the power of learning genre-independent presentations of argument units. We further apply cross-topic testing in Sect. 4.4.

4.4　Cross-Topic Settings: Testing on Unseen Topics from the Same Dataset(s)

In this section, we further assess the stacked model performance and compare it with DistilBERT, over unseen data, with a finer-grained level of cross-settings referred to as cross-topic. In this experiment, we aim to study whether the model performance over unseen topics will be improved by considering more training topics, or by considering more samples for each training topic. In other words, the analysis will reveal whether or not the diversity sampling (a wide range of topics) improves cross-topic performance.

Data. To perform these experiments, we derive a group of new datasets out of the SE, WD, and IBM datasets according to each particular classification task. The number of sentences per topic (#S/T) varies across the three datasets. However, we still need to unify the size of data for all tested combinations, as well as unifying the #S/T in every combination. By that, we analyse only the effect of diversity sampling (#T) on the model generalization to unseen topics. Hence, we fix the dataset size to 1200 sentences in each experiment. This is the maximum possible size of data that gives different combinations of #T and #S/T with respect to our corpora statistics. Apparently, this implies that a higher number of topics leads to a lower number of sentences per topic.

Experimental Set-Up. To generalize our results, We run the cross-topic over 5 runs (5 seeds) and internally over a 5-fold cross-validation setup. We report the average mean and standard deviation of the weighted precision, recall, F1 score, and accuracy on the testing set. Our 5-fold cross-validation is in terms of topics. In other words, the training set covers 80% of the topics and the remaining unseen topics are in the testing set.

Evaluation. In the following, we present the obtained results in Table 12 and Table 13 for argument identification and argument unit classification respectively. For argument identification, the evaluation results prove that the stacking model performance is consistent over the different sets of topics: W-F1 score averages between 0.810 to 0.893, and the accuracy ranges from 0.813 to 0.895. Similarly, in the unit classification task, the W-F1 averages between 0.801 to 0.858, and accuracy ranges from 0.80 to 0.855.

These findings suggest that the ensemble learning stacking approach is outperforming DistilBERT in all the cases with W-F1 score approximately +10% for argument identification and up to +5% for argument unit classification. Moreover, the former reported a lower variance in the standard deviation for almost all tested cases. This is in line with the findings of [10] who found that 100 instances of BERT is remarkably consistent in their in-distribution generalization accuracy, while they varied dramatically in their out-of-distribution generalization performance. Therefore, since BERT-like model (DistilBERT in our case) is less stable to completely unseen data, the stacked approach gets a valuable impact on the model robustness in such out-of-distribution or cross-domain scenarios. Moreover, according to Zhang et al. [35], BERT only exploit plain context-sensitive features such as character or word embeddings. It rarely consider incorporating structured semantic information which can provide rich semantics for language representation.

In terms of the impact of #T and #S/T, the weighted F1 score has been improved by increasing the #T in the training set for the argument identification task. However, the opposite behavior is observed concerning the argument unit classification task: i.e., increasing the #T decreased the weighted F1 score. We explain this contrast by the influence of the vocabulary employed in each task. In fact, the structure of arguments may differ according to the discussed topic.

Table 12. Model assessment in cross-topic experiments for argument identification task. #S/T: number of Sentences/Topic, #T: number of Topics

			W-Precision		W-Recall		W-F1 score		Accuracy	
#S/T	#T	Model	Mean	Std	Mean	Std	Mean	Std	Mean	Std
4	300	stacked model	**0.892**	±0.019	**0.895**	±0.019	**0.893**	±0.021	**0.895**	±0.019
		DistilBERT	0.765	±0.083	0.825	±0.03	0.794	±0.052	0.825	±0.03
6	200	stacked model	**0.855**	±0.009	**0.862**	±0.008	**0.858**	±0.009	**0.862**	±0.008
		DistilBERT	0.703	±0.089	0.791	±0.021	0.744	±0.036	0.791	±0.021
24	50	stacked model	**0.807**	±0.029	**0.813**	±0.026	**0.81**	±0.032	**0.813**	±0.026
		DistilBERT	0.626	±0.09	0.775	±0.03	0.693	±0.041	0.775	±0.03

For instance, we can find more statistical arguments in finance and more logical well-structured arguments in law. Therefore, ensuring distinct and diverse samples (varying topics during the training process) is important to generalize the learned patterns of argumentative text. However, for the argument unit classification, distinguishing between premise and claim is more related to the grammatical structure of sentences which does not require topic-specific vocabulary. For instance, we can use claim keywords (consequently, in fact, implies) or premise keywords (such as because, moreover, since) to distinguish between the argument components.

Table 13. Model assessment in cross-topic experiments for argument unit classification task. #S/T: number of Sentences/Topic, #T: number of Topics

			W-Precision		W-Recall		W-F1 score		Accuracy	
#S/T	#T	Model	Mean	Std	Mean	Std	Mean	Std	Mean	Std
3	400	stacked model	**0.802**	±0.013	**0.8**	±0.014	**0.801**	±0.013	**0.8**	±0.014
		DistilBERT	0.774	±0.02	0.767	±0.023	0.77	±0.022	0.767	±0.023
4	300	stacked model	**0.822**	±0.03	**0.82**	±0.032	**0.821**	±0.034	**0.82**	±0.032
		DistilBERT	0.764	±0.032	0.766	±0.031	0.765	±0.031	0.766	±0.031
6	200	stacked model	**0.825**	±0.019	**0.825**	±0.019	**0.825**	±0.02	**0.825**	±0.019
		DistilBERT	0.789	±0.02	0.786	±0.019	0.787	±0.019	0.786	±0.019
24	50	stacked model	**0.861**	±0.054	**0.855**	±0.055	**0.858**	±0.056	**0.855**	±0.055
		DistilBERT	0.847	±0.074	0.835	±0.079	0.841	±0.076	0.835	±0.079

5 Conclusion

We address in this paper two main problems of argument mining: argument identification and argument unit classification. Our study is on the sentence-level with a stacked ensemble learning approach. We aim to detect the essence of argumentative text and to assess the robustness of our model in more realistic scenarios than testing on a subset of the data known as the test split.

Furthermore, while generalization has always been an important research topic in machine learning research, the robustness and generalization of argument mining models are yet not well explored. This is a very urgent task to elevate the research in this field given the two-fold challenge it has: the lack of labeled data, and the domain dependency performance of the existing models. We believe that a formal protocol of testing the model generalization and robustness is an instant need in argumentation domain since every paper tackles it from only one angle. Most of the works suggest cross-domain models with the mean of integrating more datasets in the training process.

Therefore, in this paper, we defined sets of experiments that infer an empirical evidence on the model performance in real world applications. Based on our comparison of single-dataset learning (SDL) and multi-dataset learning (MDL), we propose that SDL is always recommended when we are confident that future dataset will be similar to the training one. Furthermore, our findings suggest that knowledge transfer is more applicable for argument identification than argument unit classification in cross-domain (out-of-distribution) setup. In terms of the latter task, the stacked model outperformed DistilBERT when tested on IBM and SE corpora. This indicates that recognizing premise and claim texts is more related to the structure of the sentence. A similar conclusion is reached in our cross-topic experiments on this particular task, where we found that the more #S/T (number of sentences per topic) we have for training, the better the stacked model generalizes to unseen topics. However, the sampling diversity (increasing the topic count #T) was essential for the argument identification task such that topic-specific vocabulary plays a crucial role.

Since the structure of the sentence made a difference in many of our experiments, we plan to test if providing a transfer learning approach (e.g., Distil-BERT) with such features, would outperform the ensemble learning approach based on this enriched knowledge. This research direction is towards the understanding of how transformers indeed work, and how we can develop them [36]. In our future work, we also plan to run joint model experiments where argument identification and argument component classification are in one sequential pipeline. We also plan to investigate more on the segmentation model that predicts the boundaries of the argument and on optimizing the combination of the base models (SVM and DistilBERT).

Acknowledgements

 The project on which this report is based was partly funded by the German Federal Ministry of Education and Research (BMBF) under the funding code 01—S20049. The author is responsible for the content of this publication.

References

1. Baker, A.: Simplicity, the Stanford Encyclopedia of Philosophy. Metaphysics Research Lab (2016)
2. Lawrence, J., Reed, C.: Argument mining: a survey. Comput. Linguist. **45**(4), 765–818 (2020)
3. Palau, R.M., Moens, M.F.: Argumentation mining: the detection, classification and structure of arguments in text. In: Proceedings of the 12th International Conference on Artificial Intelligence and Law, pp. 98–107 (2009)
4. Toulmin, S.E.: The Uses of Argument. Cambridge University Press, Cambridge (2003)
5. Stab, C., Gurevych, I.: Annotating argument components and relations in persuasive essays. In Proceedings of COLING 2014, the 25th International Conference on Computational Linguistics. Technical papers, pp. 1501–1510 (2014)
6. Song, Y., Heilman, M., Klebanov, B.B., Deane, P.: Applying argumentation schemes for essay scoring. In: Proceedings of the First Workshop on Argumentation Mining, pp. 69–78 (2014)
7. Samadi, M., Talukdar, P., Veloso, M., Blum, M.: Claimeval: integrated and flexible framework for claim evaluation using credibility of sources. In: Thirtieth AAAI Conference on Artificial Intelligence (2016)
8. Alhamzeh, A., Bouhaouel, M., Egyed-Zsigmond, E., Mitrovic, J.: Distilbert-based argumentation retrieval for answering comparative questions. In: Working Notes of CLEF (2021)
9. Al-Khatib, K., Wachsmuth, H., Hagen, M., Köhler, J., Stein, B.: Cross-domain mining of argumentative text through distant supervision. In: Proceedings of NAACL-HLT, pp. 1395–1404 (2016)
10. McCoy, R.T., Min, J., Linzen, T.: BERTs of a feather do not generalize together: Large variability in generalization across models with similar test set performance. In: Proceedings of the Third BlackboxNLP Workshop on Analyzing and Interpreting Neural Networks for NLP, pp. 217–227. Association for Computational Linguistics (2020)
11. Alhamzeh, A., Bouhaouel, M., Egyed-Zsigmond, E., Mitrović, J., Brunie, L., Kosch, H.: A stacking approach for cross-domain argument identification. In: Strauss, C., Kotsis, G., Tjoa, A.M., Khalil, I. (eds.) DEXA 2021. LNCS, vol. 12923, pp. 361–373. Springer, Cham (2021). https://doi.org/10.1007/978-3-030-86472-9_33
12. Liga, D., Palmirani, M.: Transfer learning with sentence embeddings for argumentative evidence classification (2020)
13. Wambsganss, T., Molyndris, N., Söllner, M.: Unlocking transfer learning in argumentation mining: a domain-independent modelling approach. In: 15th International Conference on Wirtschaftsinformatik (2020)

14. Zhang, W.E., Sheng, Q.Z., Alhazmi, A., Li, C.: Adversarial attacks on deep-learning models in natural language processing: a survey. ACM Trans. Intell. Syst. Technol. (TIST) **11**(3), 1–41 (2020)
15. Tzeng, E., Hoffman, J., Saenko, K., Darrell, T.: Adversarial discriminative domain adaptation. In: Proceedings of the IEEE Conference on Computer Vision and Pattern Recognition, pp. 7167–7176 (2017)
16. Schiller, B., Daxenberger, J., Gurevych, I.: Stance detection benchmark: how robust is your stance detection? KI - Künstl. Intell. **35**(3), 329–341 (2021). https://doi.org/10.1007/s13218-021-00714-w
17. Ajjour, Y., Chen, W.F., Kiesel, J., Wachsmuth, H., Stein, B.: Unit segmentation of argumentative texts. In: Proceedings of the 4th Workshop on Argument Mining, pp. 118–128 (2017)
18. Al Khatib, K., Wachsmuth, H., Kiesel, J., Hagen, M., Stein, B.: A news editorial corpus for mining argumentation strategies. In Proceedings of COLING 2016, the 26th International Conference on Computational Linguistics: Technical Papers, pp. 3433–3443 (2016)
19. Habernal, I., Gurevych, I.: Argumentation mining in user-generated web discourse. Comput. Linguist. **43**(1), 125–179 (2017)
20. Bouslama, R., Ayachi, R., Amor, N.B.: Using convolutional neural network in cross-domain argumentation mining framework. In: Ben Amor, N., Quost, B., Theobald, M. (eds.) SUM 2019. LNCS (LNAI), vol. 11940, pp. 355–367. Springer, Cham (2019). https://doi.org/10.1007/978-3-030-35514-2_26
21. Elangovan, A., He, J., Verspoor, K.: Memorization vs. generalization: quantifying data leakage in NLP performance evaluation. In: Proceedings of the 16th Conference of the European Chapter of the Association for Computational Linguistics: Main Volume, pp. 1325–1335 (2021)
22. Huan, X., Mannor, S.: Robustness and generalization. Mach. Learn. **86**(3), 391–423 (2012). https://doi.org/10.1007/s10994-011-5268-1
23. Wang, J.: Generalizing to unseen domains: a survey on domain generalization. IEEE Trans. Knowl. Data Eng. (2022)
24. Stab, C., Gurevych, I.: Parsing argumentation structures in persuasive essays. Comput. Linguist. **43**(3), 619–659 (2017)
25. Stab, C.: Argumentative Writing Support by Means of Natural Language Processing, p. 208 (2017)
26. Aharoni, E.: A benchmark dataset for automatic detection of claims and evidence in the context of controversial topics. In: Proceedings of the First Workshop on Argumentation Mining, pp. 64–68 (2014)
27. Sagi, O., Rokach, L.: Ensemble learning: a survey. Wiley Interdis. Rev.: Data Min. Knowl. Discovery **8**(4), e1249 (2018)
28. Moens, M.F., Boiy, E., Palau, R.M., Reed, C.: Automatic detection of arguments in legal texts. In: Proceedings of the 11th International Conference on Artificial Intelligence and Law, pp. 225–230 (2007)
29. Stab, C., Gurevych, I.: Identifying argumentative discourse structures in persuasive essays. In: Proceedings of the 2014 Conference on Empirical Methods in Natural Language Processing (EMNLP), pp. 46–56 (2014)
30. Sanh, V., Debut, L., Chaumond, J., Wolf, T.: Distilbert, a distilled version of bert: smaller, faster, cheaper and lighter. arXiv preprint. arXiv:1910.01108 (2019)
31. Devlin, J., Chang, M.W., Lee, K., Toutanova, K.: Bert: pre-training of deep bidirectional transformers for language understanding. arXiv preprint. arXiv:1810.04805 (2018)

32. Ryu, M., Lee, K.: Knowledge distillation for bert unsupervised domain adaptation. arXiv preprint. arXiv:2010.11478 (2020)
33. Loshchilov, I., Hutter, F.: Decoupled weight decay regularization. arXiv preprint. arXiv:1711.05101 (2017)
34. De Winter, J.C.F.: Using the student's t-test with extremely small sample sizes. Pract. Assess. Res. Eval. **18**(1), 10 (2013)
35. Zhang, Z., et al.: Semantics-aware BERT for language understanding. In: Proceedings of the AAAI Conference on Artificial Intelligence, vol. 34, no. 05, pp. 9628–9635 (2020)
36. Rogers, A., Kovaleva, O., Rumshisky, A.: A primer in bertology: what we know about how bert works. Trans. Assoc. Comput. Linguist. **8**, 842–866 (2020)

A Pattern Mining Framework for Improving Billboard Advertising Revenue

P. Revanth Rathan[1]($\boxtimes$), P. Krishna Reddy[1], and Anirban Mondal[2]

[1] IIIT Hyderabad, Hyderabad, India
revanth.parvathaneni@research.iiit.ac.in, pkreddy@iiit.ac.in
[2] Ashoka University, Sonipat, India
anirban.mondal@ashoka.edu.in

Abstract. Billboard advertisement is one of the dominant modes of traditional outdoor advertisements. A billboard operator manages the ad slots of a set of billboards. Normally, a user traversal is exposed to multiple billboards. Given a set of billboards, there is an opportunity to improve the revenue of the billboard operator by satisfying the advertising demands of an increased number of clients and ensuring that a user gets exposed to different ads on the billboards during the traversal. In this paper, we propose a framework to improve the revenue of the billboard operator by employing transactional modeling in conjunction with pattern mining. Our main contributions are three-fold. First, we introduce the problem of billboard advertisement allocation for improving the billboard operator revenue. Second, we propose an efficient user trajectory-based transactional framework using coverage pattern mining for improving the revenue of the billboard operator. Third, we conduct a performance study with a real dataset to demonstrate the effectiveness of our proposed framework.

Keywords: billboard advertisement · data mining · pattern mining · transactional modeling · user trajectory · ad revenue

1 Introduction

Billboard advertisement is among the dominant modes of traditional outdoor advertisements. Notably, outdoor ads constitute a $500 billion market around the world [4]. In fact, billboards are the most widely used medium for outdoor ads with a market share of about 65%, and 80% people notice them while driving [1].

A given billboard operator (BO) rents/owns and manages a set of billboards by allocating the ads of *clients* on the billboards in lieu of a cost, while *users* view the billboard ads during transit. Observe that budget is a critical factor for the client. For example, the average cost of renting a billboard ad space in New York can run into thousands of dollars per month [31].

© Springer-Verlag GmbH Germany, part of Springer Nature 2022
A. Hameurlain and A. M. Tjoa (Eds.): *Transactions on Large-Scale Data- and Knowledge-Centered Systems LII*, LNCS 13470, pp. 127–147, 2022.
https://doi.org/10.1007/978-3-662-66146-8_6

The key goal of *BO* is to maximize its revenue by allocating ads of clients on billboards. This paper introduces the problem of *efficient* billboard ad allocation to clients for improving the revenue of *BO* by assigning ads to billboards such that a typical user is exposed to several *distinct* ads in her trajectory as far as possible. We refer to this problem as the **B**illboard **AL**location (**BAL**) problem.

Existing works have primarily focused on the selection of billboard locations by means of analysing trajectory data [5,22,28,31]. Our work fundamentally differs from existing works as follows. While existing works try to improve billboard advertising from the clients' perspective, we focus on improving the revenue of *BO*. We also address the requirements of *multiple* clients by approaching the problem as a pattern mining problem.

In this paper, we propose a framework, which is called Billboard Allocation Framework (BAF) to improve the revenue of *BO* by extending the notions of transactional modeling and *coverage*. In BAF, each user trajectory is modeled as a transaction. Given a transactional dataset of user trajectories, the issue is to determine the potential combinations of billboards such that each combination *covers* a required number of unique trajectories (users) by minimizing *overlap*. Such combinations could be allocated to different clients based on the requirement. However, for determining potential combinations of billboards from m billboards, we need to examine $2^m - 1$ combinations, which leads to a combinatorial explosion problem.

To tackle the billboard allocation problem, we have exploited the opportunity of extending the framework of Coverage Pattern (CP) mining [10,27], which can be extracted from transactional databases by exploiting apriori based pruning property. The notion of CPs was proposed to extract transactional coverage value of distinct sets of data items or patterns from the given transactional database. The CPs from the given transactional databse can be extracted based on the specified threshold values of relative frequency (RF), coverage support (CS) and overlap ratio (OR) parameters. The concept of CPs can be extended to extract the potential combinations of billboards from user trajectory data in an efficient manner. BAF comprises the formation of transactions from user trajectory data and a CP-based billboard views allocation approach. In BAF, we extract CPs from transactions, which are formed by processing user trajectory data. Each CP is assigned with the values of coverage support (CS) and the overlap ratio (OR). Notably, CS of a CP indicates the number of unique transactions and the value of OR represents the extent of overlap, which is equal to the number of repetitions among the transactions covered by CP. We propose the mapping function to convert the CS of the extracted CPs to views and a ranking function to order the CPs. Finally, we allocate the generated CPs (i.e., a set of billboards) to the clients subject to their requirements.

Our key contributions are three-fold:

- We introduce the billboard allocation problem (BAL) for improving the billboard operator revenue.
- We propose an efficient user trajectory-based transactional framework (BAF) using coverage pattern mining for addressing the billboard allocation problem.

– We conducted a performance study with a real dataset to demonstrate the effectiveness of the proposed framework.

In our short paper in [25], we have made a preliminary effort to present the billboard allocation problem and BAF. In this paper, we have extended the literature survey and improved the readability of paper by adding the algorithm and illustrative example. We also carried out extensive performance experiments with additional parameters and metrics.

The remainder of this paper is organized as follows. In Sect. 2, we discuss related works and background. In Sect. 3, we explain the proposed framework of the problem. In Sect. 4, we present our proposed ad allocation framework (BAF). In Sect. 5, we report the performance study. Finally, we conclude in Sect. 6 with directions for future work.

2   Related Work and Background

We first provide an overview of existing works in this area followed by background of coverage patterns.

2.1   Related Work

Influence maximization (IM) problem originally proposed in [8,26] aimed to find the k-sized subset among all the nodes in a network for maximizing the influence spread. The work in [15] had proven this problem to be NP-hard. The work in [19] provides a survey of existing studies on IM.

Recently, the traditional IM problem had been extended to location-aware IM problem by additionally considering the knowledge of the spatial dimension and budgeted influence maximization (BIM) problem. The work in [18] proposed two greedy schemes for the effective computation of the location-aware IM problem. The work in [12] proposed both exact and approximate algorithms to obtain top-k trajectories, which maximize the influence based on the user's locations in the trajectory database. The proposal in [6] aimed to find a set of nodes that maximizes the expected number of influenced users under the constraint that the total cost of the users in the set of nodes is not larger than the budget. Furthermore, it presented new bound estimation techniques and new node selection strategies to solve budgeted influence maximization problem.

An algorithm based on greedy heuristics was proposed in [20] to compute the k-billboard location set with the most influence. An approach was proposed for the optimal placement of the billboards in [13]. In the above work, optimal placement indicates reaching the maximum number of potentially interested users. The work in [23] proposed an advertising strategy based on multi-agent deep reinforcement learning for determining how to switch the advertising content in each digital billboard to maximize the profit. The proposal in [14] introduced a dynamic optimization models for displaying digital billboard advertisements at the right time and place. They provided an optimal solution for digital billboard configuration with a greater coverage of the target audience compared to the state-of-the-art static models. The work in [22] designed a system called *SmartAdP* to compute and visualize the optimal placement of billboards.

Notably, the adaptive version of the above-proposed IM approaches tries to efficiently estimate the maximum influence billboard set in a network and allocates it to the client. Observe that there is no notion of the client's requirements in the works mentioned above. In essence, these works try to optimally allocate the maximum influenced set to the client, thereby leading to a decrease in the revenue for *BO*.

Research efforts are also being made to find the optimal set of billboards (in the billboard advertisement scenario) based on the spatial trajectories of the users [28,31,32]. The approach proposed in [31] uses a database of trajectories and a budget constraint L to find a set of billboards within a budget such that the ads placed on the selected billboards influence the most significant number of trajectories. It divides the billboards into a set of clusters based on the overlap and maximizes the unique views (influence) in each cluster with a specific budget using dynamic programming and outputs the combined output from each cluster. The work in [28] constructed a quantitative model to characterize influence spread by comprehensively considering three key factors, i.e., advertisement topics, traffic conditions (traffic flow and average speed), and mobility transition with the goal of maximizing the total expected advertisement influence spread. However, it does not consider the budget of the user and the billboard's cost. The proposal in [32] aimed to find a set of billboards that have the maximum influence under the budget. In this work, they introduced a non-sub modular influence model and proposed an optimized method to compute the influence of billboards on the user traversals.

Incidentally, pattern mining is one of the tasks of data mining. Pattern mining involves extracting interesting associations that exist in the given transactional databases. Some of the interesting measures that capture the associations w.r.t. the other items in the patterns include frequency, periodicity, utility, coverage, sequential, fuzzy, etc. Research efforts had been made in the literature to find the patterns with the above mentioned interesting measures in the underlying database [5,16,17,27,29,30].

The work in [27] proposed a model of coverage patterns (CPs) and a methodology to extract them from transactional databases. It demonstrated the value of using CPs by considering the problem of banner advertisements placement in e-commerce web sites. As an example, given the pages of a website, a CP is a set of pages that are visited by a certain percentage of the visitors. The CPs discovered from click-stream data facilitated the publisher in satisfying the demands of multiple advertisers. Alternative approaches to extract CPs were proposed in [10]. The proposal in [10] discussed CP extraction approaches based on pattern growth techniques. The notion of coverage patterns has been extended to improve the performance of search engine advertising [7] and visibility computation [9].

As discussed in Sect. 1, our work fundamentally differs from existing works since our work addresses the issue of improving the revenue of *BO*. Moreover, existing works address the requirement of only *one* client, while we address the requirement of *multiple* clients. Furthermore, we approach the problem as a pattern mining problem, while existing works pose it as an optimization problem.

2.2 Background About Coverage Patterns

We now explain the concept of coverage patterns (CPs) [10, 27]. CPs are characterized with the notions of relative frequency (RF), coverage support (CS) and overlap ratio (OR). Given a transactional database D, each transaction is a subset of a set I of m items $\{i_1, i_2, i_3, \ldots, i_r, \ldots, i_m\}$ where i_r represents r^{th} item $\forall r \in [1, m]$. T^{i_r} denotes the set of transactions in which item i_r is present. The fraction of transactions containing a given item i_r is designated as *Relative Frequency RF(i_r)* of i_r. $RF(i_r) = |T^{i_r}|/|D|$. An item is considered as *frequent* if its relative frequency is greater than that of a threshold value designated as *minRF*. A pattern P is a subset of items in I i.e., $P \subseteq I$ where $P = \{i_p, i_q, \ldots, i_r\}$ and $1 \leq RF(i_p) \leq RF(i_q) \leq \ldots RF(i^r)$. *Coverage Set* CSet($P$) of a pattern $P = \{i^p, i_q, \ldots, i_r\}$ is the set of all the transactions that contain at least one item from the pattern P i.e., $CSet(P) = T^{i_p} \cup T^{i_q}, \ldots, \cup T^{i_r}$. *Coverage Support* CS($P$) is the ratio of the size of CSet(P) to the size of D i.e., $CS(P) = |CSet(P)| / |D|$.

To add a new item to the pattern P such that CS increases significantly, the notion of *overlap ratio* is introduced. (This is possible in the case when the number of transactions, which are common to the new item and the pattern P, is low.) *Overlap ratio OR(P)* of a pattern P is the ratio of the number of transactions that are common between CSet($P - i^r$) and T^{i_r} to the number of transactions in T^{i_r}, i.e., $OR(P) = (|CSet(P-i_r) \cap (T^{i_r})|)/(|T^{i_r}|)$. A high CS value indicates more transactions and a low OR value means less repetitions among the transactions. A pattern is *interesting* if its CS is greater than or equal to the user-specified minimum CS threshold value (i.e., *minCS*) and its OR is less than or equal to user-specified maximum OR threshold value (i.e., *maxOR*). Given *minRF*, *minCS* and *maxOR*, pattern $P = \{i_p, i_q, \ldots, i_r\}$ is regarded as a *coverage pattern CP* if $RF(i_k) \geq minRF \ \forall i_k \in P$, $CS(P) \geq minCS$ and $OR(P) \leq maxOR$.

The notion of *overlap ratio* satisfies sorted closure property [21]. By exploiting sorted closure property of *overlap ratio*, a level-wise apriori-based approach has been proposed in [27] and pattern-growth-based approach is proposed in [10] for extracting all CPs from D, given *minRF*, *minCS* and *maxOR* values.

Illustrative Example of Coverage Patterns: Table 1 represents the transactional dataset D. TID in the Table 1 represents the transaction id. Let us assume the values for *minRF*, *minCS* and *maxOR* are 0.4, 0.7 and 0.5 respectively. Let us take the pattern $\{b, e\}$. CS of the pattern represents the fraction of transaction, which has at least one of the item of the pattern. From Table 1, we observe that apart from transaction whose TID is 10, all other transactions contains one of the items from above pattern. Hence, CS is 0.9. OR technically represents the fraction of new transactions added to the coverage set by adding an item w.r.t. the number of transaction containing that item. Here in pattern $\{b, e\}$, only 2 patterns contains both the items in the pattern out of 4 patterns, which has item e. Hence, OR is 0.5. In the similar way, we can compute all the patterns, which are eligible to be a coverage pattern. Table 2 depicts all the enumerated coverage patterns from D with the specified threshold values.

Table 1. Transactional Database

TID	Items	TID	Items
1	a, b, c	6	b, d
2	a, c, e	7	b, d
3	a, c, e	8	b, e
4	a, c, d	9	b, e
5	b, d, f	10	a, b

Table 2. Extracted Coverage Patterns

Pattern	CS	OR	Pattern	CS	OR
b	0.7	0	a, e	0.7	0.5
b, a	1	0.4	c, d	0.7	0.25
b, c	1	0.25	d, e	0.8	0
b, e	0.9	0.5	a, d ,e	1	0.5
a, d	0.9	0.25	c, d, e	0.9	0.5

3 Proposed Framework of the Problem

Billboards are visible road-side ad hoardings. Consistent with real-world scenarios, we assume that only *one* advertisement is displayed in a given billboard at a specific point in time. A given *billboard operator (BO)* rents/owns the billboards in a particular region. *Clients* wish to display their ads on the billboards. *BO* assigns the sets of billboards to the clients for a particular cost, namely *billboard cost*. *User trajectory* is a sequence of GPS locations traversed by a given user. If a user stops at any location for more than a threshold amount of time, we consider her trajectory after the stoppage as a new user trajectory.

Views of a billboard are defined as the total number of user trajectories, which are influenced by the billboard. We consider that a user trajectory is influenced by the billboard if it passes through the sector of radius λ and angle θ in the vicinity of the billboard (Here, the sector is drawn using the centroid of the billboard as the centre). For example, from Fig. 1, the user trajectory ut_1 is influenced by the billboard b_1, but the user trajectory ut_2 is not influenced by b_1. This is because ut_1 traverses through the visible sector of b_1, which is not the case for ut_2. Each billboard has unique values of λ and θ, which depends on the dimensions of the billboard (like, height and size of the billboard) and the neighbourhood. Furthermore, we assume the existence of conversion schemes [2,3], which convert the budget of the client to the views of the billboard.

Consider a set of m billboards B $\{b_1, b_2, .., b_m\}$ and a set $C = \{c_1, c_2, .., c_n\}$ of n clients, where c_i represents a client's unique identifier. Let $t(c_i)$ be the budget of client c_i, while $v(c_i)$ is the threshold number of views corresponding to $t(c_i)$. Moreover, $v(b_i)$ is the number of user trajectories, which viewed billboard b_i.

The **Billboard ALlocation (BAL)** problem aims to improve the revenue of BO by allocating different sets of billboards to the maximum number of clients in set C by satisfying clients' budget constraint. The sum of all views of the billboards in the set s_i i.e., $\{b_1, b_2, ..., b_{|s_i|}\}$ is equal to $\sum_{k=1}^{|s_i|} v(b_k)$. Mathematically, we can allocate the billboards set s_i to client c_i if

$$\sum_{k=1}^{|s_i|} v(b_k) \geq v(c_i) \tag{1}$$

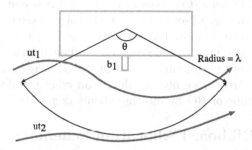

Fig. 1. Spatial influence region of a given billboard

From Eq. 1, we can guarantee that the total number of user trajectories, which views the ad of the client is always greater than or equal to the views specified by the client c_i i.e., $v(c_i)$.

The issue is to enumerate the set of billboards and allocate it to clients by satisfying his/her constraints. Since, BO costs the billboard based on the number of user trajectories visits, it is not beneficial for the clients if the user encounters the same advertisement in the billboards during their trajectory. In addition, the goal of BO is to reach maximum number of clients. Since each user trajectory is exposed to multiple billboards, it is advisable for BO to allocate different advertisements to user during her trajectory. From the above discussion, the main issue is to find the set of billboards by minimizing the repetition of user trajectories between them. We can capture this scenario using the notion of *Overlap*.

The billboard set s_i assigned to the client c_i should have *Overlap* less than or equal to the threshold maximum overlap value (maxOV), i.e., $Overlap(s_i, UT) \leq maxOV$. By using this *overlap constraint*, BO ensures that the client's advertisement in the billboard is guaranteed to be viewed by at least a minimum number of *distinct* user trajectories.

Multiple candidate sets may qualify with the given budget ($t(c_i)$) and overlap (maxOV) constraints. In this regard, we have to address two key issues, namely *extraction* and *allocation* issues. Extraction issue deals with the enumeration of sets of billboards. Allocation problem deals with the allocation of enumerated sets of billboards to appropriate clients.

Now we define the BAL problem as follows:

BAL Problem: Consider a billboard operator BO, a set UT of user trajectories, a set of m billboards B $\{b_1, b_2, \ldots, b_m\}$ and a set C of n clients such that $C = \{c_1, c_2, \ldots, c_n\}$. The billboard operator (BO) has to assign a set of billboards from $S = \{s_1, s_2, \ldots, s_o\}$, where each candidate set s_i comprises a set of billboards, to maximum number of clients in the set C such that $\sum_{k=1}^{|s_j|} v(b_k) \geq v(c_i)$ and $Overlap(s_j, UT) \leq maxOV$, $\forall s_j \in S$ and $\forall c_i \in C$ to improve the revenue.

The set S in BAL problem indicates sets of all possible combinations of billboard locations. Observe that computing the set S is computation-intensive as it depends upon the size of set B. Let m be the size of set B. As the value of m increases, time taken to compute the set S exponentially increases since we need to compute $2^m - 1$ potential combinations of billboard locations. Furthermore, arbitrary allocation of the combinations of billboard locations does not improve the revenue of BO. Hence, we need to devise an efficient allocation framework to improve the revenue of BO by meeting clients demands.

4   Proposed Billboard Allocation Scheme

In this section, we present our proposed scheme.

4.1   Basic Idea

Normally, in the context of databases, a transaction [11] is defined as an atomic task, which consists of several sub-tasks that are performed either in entirety or not performed at all. A transaction is employed to comprehend the real-world task at a certain granularity. Similarly, in the proposed BAL problem scenario, a user views a set of billboards during his trajectory. We consider a user trajectory, which consists of views (locations) if billboard as an atomic entity. As a result, there is an opportunity to model user trajectories as a transactional database. Once it is converted into a transactional database, we get the opportunity of extending pattern mining approaches such as coverage pattern mining [10, 27] to propose improved billboard allocation framework by exploiting apriori based pruning strategy to tackle exponential complexity of enumeration problem discussed in Sect. 3.

We refer to the proposed framework as Billboard Allocation Framework (**BAF**). The overview of BAF is as follows. First, we preprocess the user trajectory data to get transactions. Next, we generate CPs from the transaction data. Each CP is assigned with the values of coverage support (CS) and the overlap ratio (OR). Notably, CS of a CP indicates the number of unique transactions. However, for allocation, we require the number of views of a CP. To compute views of a given CP, we propose the mapping function to convert the CS of the extracted CPs to views. We also propose a ranking function to order the CPs based on the proposed uniqueness measure. Then we propose an efficient framework to allocate the generated CPs (i.e., a set of billboards) to the clients subject to their requirements.

The proposed BAF also provides an opportunity to extract potential CPs in an *offline* manner. We can use the extracted CPs towards the efficient allocation of billboards in an online manner. In BAF, we consider the notion of overlap ratio used in CPs to capture the overlap of the billboard set.

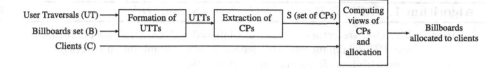

Fig. 2. Proposed Billboard Allocation Framework (BAF)

4.2   Proposed BAF

Figure 2 depicts a diagrammatic representation of BAF. BAF comprises three steps: (1) Formation of user trajectory transactions ($UTTs$), (2) Extraction of coverage patterns (CPs) and (3) Computing views of CPs and allocation. Algorithm 1 shows the proposed BAF framework.

1. Formation of user trajectory transactions ($UTTs$): Here, the input is a set of user trajectories UT and billboards B and output is UTTs. We convert each UT into UTT by including billboard locations covered by UT (see Line 1 of Algorithm 1).

2. Extraction of CPs: Based on $minRF$, $minCS$ and $maxOR$, we employ the existing CP mining algorithm proposed in [27] and extract S (see Line 2). Note that we use the notion of maximum overlap ratio ($maxOR$) defined in [27] to capture the notion of $maxOV$ in BAL problem.

3. Computing views of CPs and allocation: It consists of three sub-steps.
(i) Computing views and uniqueness rank of a CP: We compute the number of user views for each CP in S. CS of a CP is the effective number of unique users influenced by the billboards in the pattern. Let s_i be a CP, $|T_{b_i}|$ be the number of $UTTs$ influenced by the billboard b_i and $views(s_i)$ denote the views of s_i. Then $views(s_i) = \sum_{\forall b_i \in s_i} |T_{b_i}|$ (see Line 4 of Algorithm 1).

Notably, the number of views computed in Step (i) includes the repeated views. Since a large number of CPs are extracted from the $UTTs$, when the views of several patterns are equal, it is beneficial to allocate the pattern with the maximum number of distinct views. Given two patterns having the same number of views, a pattern is considered to have more unique views if it has more CS and less OR. For a given s_i, we capture the uniqueness of a pattern with uniqueness rank heuristic $U(s_i)$, which equals $(CS(s_i) * (1 - OR(s_i)))$ (see Line 5).

(ii) Computing views required by clients: BO trades the views of the billboard with the budget provided by the client. We employ marketing conversion schemes such as cost per thousand impressions [2,3] to convert the budget to views as follows: $v_j = convert(t_j)$, where v_j is the views demanded by client for budget t_j and $convert()$ is the conversion function decided by BO (see Line 8).
(iii) Allocation: Several allocation methods are possible. We now present one of the methods. We sort S in the decreasing order of both number of views and uniqueness (see Line 10). We sort the list of the clients C in the decreasing order of the required views (see Line 11). Each client c_j is allocated with the

---

Algorithm 1: BAF(UT, B, C, $minRF$, $minCS$, $maxOR$)

Input : UT: User trajectories; B: set of billboards; C $<c_j, t_j>$: set of clients; $minRF$: minimum relative frequency; $minCS$: minimum coverage support; $maxOR$: maximum overlap ratio

Output: M: Mapping of the candidate sets to the clients

1 Form UTTs from UT using B.
2 S = Extract_CPs(UTTs, $minRF$, $minCS$, $maxOR$)
3 **foreach** $s_i \in S$ **do**
4       $views(s_i) = \sum_{\forall b_i \in s_i} |T_{b_i}|$
5       $U(s_i) = (CS(s_i) * (1 - OR(s_i)))$
6   Update s_i with $<s_i, views(s_i), U(s_i)>$

7 **foreach** $c_j \in C$ **do**
8       $v_j = convert(t_j)$
9   Update $<c_j, t_j>$ with $<c_j, v_j, t_j>$

10 Sort S in the descending order of $views(s_i)$ and $U(s_i)$
11 Sort C in the descending order of v_j
12 **foreach** $c_j \in C$ **do**
13   CP = $\arg\min_{s_i}(views(s_i) - v_j)$
14   **if** *CP is empty* **then**
15   break
16       $M[c_j]$ = CP
17   R $\leftarrow$ { s_i / $\forall b \in$ CP, $b \in s_i$ }
18   S $\leftarrow$ S - R

19 **return** M

---

eligible candidate set s_i, which satisfies the requirement of the client c_j, i.e., $views(s_i) \geq v_j$. Multiple candidate sets may satisfy the above requirement. Hence, we allocate the s_i to c_j, which satisfies the above condition and has the minimum difference of views required by c_j and views of s_i (see Line 13). After allocation, we need to remove all the sets where the allocated billboards are present (see Lines 17–18). The above procedure continues until all the clients are allocated with the potential candidate sets, or remaining candidate sets are unable to satisfy the clients.

4.3 Illustrative Example

For a better understanding of our approach, we now present a working example of the allocation step of BAF. In the allocation step, we first sort the generated patterns in descending order of views and uniqueness. Sorted coverage patterns are shown in Table 3. Next, we sort the clients in the descending order of the views requested (see Table 4).

Observe that during the allocation step, we first try to allocate the corresponding pattern to the client with the highest requested views. Since the client

Table 3. Details of the generated CPs

CP	CS	OR	uniqueness (U)	Views
cp_1	0.8	0.2	0.64	945
cp_2	0.8	0.5	0.40	945
cp_3	0.6	0.2	0.48	875
cp_4	0.6	0.5	0.30	745

Table 4. Details of the Client

Client	Views requested
c_1	945
c_2	930
c_3	900

c_1 has the highest views, we try to allocate the pattern with at least 945 views. The patterns cp_1 and cp_2 satisfy the requirement of c_1, but cp_1 has the highest value of U. Hence, we allocate the pattern cp_1 to the client c_1. Next, we try to allocate a pattern to the client c_2. Observe that no pattern in Table 3 has the same amount of views specified by the client c_2. Hence, we try to search for the pattern with the views that are greater than that of the requested views. Consequently, we allocate the pattern cp_2 to the client c_2. To satisfy the client c_3, we have to search Table 3 for the pattern, which has not been previously allocated such that the patterns should have views greater than or equal to 900. Since no such pattern exists in Table 3, the client c_3 cannot be satisfied. Hence, the allocation step terminates because the remaining candidate sets are unable to satisfy the clients.

4.4   Time and Space Complexity

In this section, we present the detailed analysis of space and time complexity of every step in BAF framework.

First step is the formation of $UTTs$. The time complexity for this step is $O(|UT|)$. Here $|UT|$ represents the number of user traversals i.e., the size of the dataset. Second step is the extraction of the coverage patterns from $UTTs$. Coverage pattern mining algorithm is one-pass algorithm, which means a single scan to the complete database is sufficient to mine the patterns. The time complexity for second step is $O(|UT|)$. We do the first two steps i.e., the formation of $UTTs$ and generation of coverage patterns from them in an offline manner. Performing an algorithm offline implies that we can execute the algorithm in advance and can materialize the knowledge in the repository. We can use the materialized knowledge for performing multiple client requests without carrying out the computation from scratch for each request.

The time complexity for the third step in the algorithm is as follows: (i) computing the views and uniqueness of each billboard set (i.e., a pattern) and convert the budget of the client into the views is $O(|S|) + O(|C|)$ (ii) sorting the extracted coverage patterns and clients is $O(|S| * log(|S|)) + O(|C| * log|C|$ (iii) iterate through each billboard set and allocate it to clients such that it satisfies their requirements is $O(|S|)$. In general, $|S| \gg |C|$. Hence, the **time complexity** of Algorithm 1 comes to $O(|S| * log(|S|))$. Moreover, the **space** required for Algorithm 1 is equal to the space for storing all extracted potential billboard sets (coverage patterns) and the mapping of client and billboard set.

5 Performance Evaluation

We conducted experiments on an Intel Core i7-7500U CPU @ 2.70GHz × 4 PC with 8GB RAM running Ubuntu 18.04 Linux. We implemented the approaches in Python. Our experiment used Microsoft's *GeoLife* [33] real dataset. The dataset contains 17,621 trajectories with a total distance of 1,292,951 km and a total duration of 50,176 h. In this work, we considered 13,971 trajectories within Beijing's Fifth Ring Road. Figure 3 depicts the heat maps of these trajectories in the GeoLife dataset. We used OpenStreetMap[1] for Beijing to obtain the road network. First, we mapped each trajectory of the user to the road network using a map-matching tool Graphhopper[2]. Then we used nominatim[3] to obtain the corresponding sequence of edge IDs of road segments as an user trajectory.

The GeoLife dataset does not contain information about billboard locations. Since billboards are typically placed in regions with relatively more user trajectories due to cost reasons, we placed billboard locations in the GeoLife dataset only in road segments, where the number of user trajectories exceeds a pre-specified threshold. We assume that a billboard influences a user trajectory if the edge ID corresponding to the billboard exists in the sequence of edge IDs of the user trajectory. We set the billboard's cost to be proportional to the frequency of user trajectories in the road segment containing the billboard.

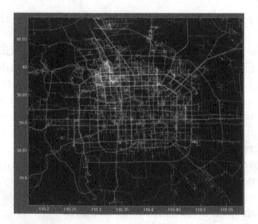

Fig. 3. Heat maps of user trajectories in GeoLife dataset

[1] https://www.openstreetmap.org.
[2] https://graphhopper.com/api/1/docs/map-matching/.
[3] https://nominatim.openstreetmap.org/.

Table 5. Parameters of the performance study

Parameter	Default	Variations
Number of clients (N_C)	20	5, 10, 15, 25, 30
Number of available billboards (N_B)	50	10 ,20, 30, 40
$maxOR$	0.5	0, 0.1, 0.2, 0.3, 0.4
$minCS$	0.1	

We selected the performance study parameters to closely reflect real-world scenarios based on existing works [7, 31]. Table 5 summarizes the performance study parameters. Our performance metrics include execution time (ET), the number of billboards allocated (BA), the number of distinct clients reached (CA), the number of views assigned (VA) and Ad Repeatability (AR). Notably, ET concerns the time required for the allocation of the billboard set to the clients. Incidentally, in our proposed framework, we compute the knowledge of coverage patterns in an *offline* manner and use them to allocate billboards at run-time. ET does not include the time required to generate coverage patterns since these patterns are generated offline.

The metric BA computes the number of billboards utilized in the process of allocation. A higher value of BA indicates better utilization of available billboards. CA captures the number of clients, whose requirements are satisfied i.e., the number of clients allocated with the set of billboards. A higher value of CA is better as it satisfies the demands of more clients, thereby contributing to higher revenue. VA is the number of *unique views* assigned in the process of allocation. As discussed in Sect. 3, a higher value of VA implies more revenue for the billboard operator.

AR captures the notion of *overlap* (see Sect. 3). To compute overlap, we introduce the notion of *user-level diversity (UD)*, which indicates the number of times a user encounters the same ad during her trajectory. A low value of AR implies more efficient utilization of billboards, which indicates improved user-level diversity. In this paper, our main aim is to reach the maximum number of distinct user trajectories. In this work, we compute AR as the fraction of views corresponding to the same ad, which is traversed by the user more than once. AR of the set CS of clients satisfied and UD of the client c_i after allocating the billboard set s_i are computed as follows:

$$AR = \frac{\sum_{c_i in CS} UD(c_i)}{VA} \tag{2}$$

$$where, UD(c_i) = \begin{cases} \sum_{\forall b_i, b_j \in s_i, b_i \neq b_j} |T^{b_i} \cap T^{b_j}|, & |s_i| \geq 2 \\ 0. & \text{otherwise.} \end{cases}$$

Recall that given a set of billboards with their respective costs and user trajectory data, the approach proposed in [31] determines the maximum influence set within a pre-specified budget (see Sect. 2). However, it satisfies only a single client. Hence, as reference, for the purpose of meaningful comparison, we adapted the approach proposed in [31] as follows. First, we represent the views of the billboard in terms of budget. We represent the cost of a given billboard b as $views(b)/1000$ [2,3]. We use the notion of overlap discussed in Sect. 2.2 as the metric to divide the billboards into clusters such that the overlap between the clusters is always less than a pre-specified threshold. We sort the clients in descending order of budget (in terms of views). Second, using the approach proposed in [31], we compute the billboard set with maximum influence within the budget of the first client (after sorting). We allocate the computed billboard set to the client if the aggregate views of the set of billboards are greater than 90% of the views specified by the client since this approach maximizes the views within the budget. We remove billboards, which are allocated to the previous client, and execute the approach as mentioned above for every client until we process all of the clients or until all of the billboards have been allocated. In this work, we refer to this improved reference approach as partsel framework (**PSF**). Notably, for all the approaches, we generated the budget of clients randomly in the range between the values of $minCS$ and $|UTT|$.

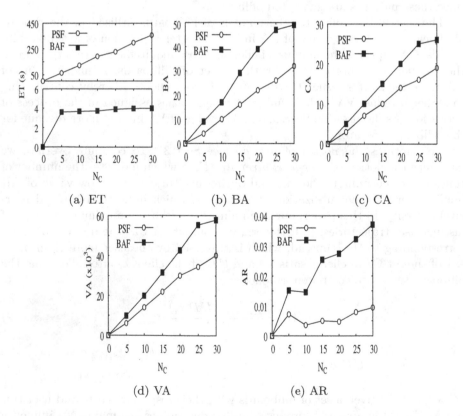

Fig. 4. Effect of varying the number of clients for GeoLife dataset

In our proposed BAF, we divide the user trajectories into multiple user trajectory transactions ($UTTs$) based on billboard locations. In particular, we deployed the *parallel C-Mine* algorithm [24] to obtain all candidate coverage patterns from $UTTs$ with the value of $minRF = 0$ for GeoLife dataset in an *offline* manner.

5.1 Effect of Varying the Number of Clients

Figure 4 depicts the results for varying the number N_C of clients. As N_C increases, ET increases for both schemes. This occurs because the allocation step should run for every client. Observe that ET for allocating the clients in BAF is much lower than that of PSF. This occurs because most of the computations in case of BAF (i.e., computation of coverage patterns) is done offline. In contrast, for PSF, there is no scope for performing any offline computations in advance, hence the allocation step needs to perform all the required computations for every client during run-time, thereby resulting in higher values of ET in case of PSF. Observe that in the results of Fig. 4b, the billboards allocated in BAF are always greater than the number of billboards allocated in PSF. The result indicates that BAF has better utilization of available billboards than PSF since it uses almost all the billboards for allocation, thereby leading to an increase in revenue for BO.

From the results in Fig. 4c, observe that BAF satisfies all the clients until $N_C=25$. In BAF, more than 95% of the billboards are allocated after satisfying the 26th client. However, most of the clients are not satisfied with the billboard set provided by PSF. This occurs because PSF tries to maximize the influence within the budget, and the maximum influence it can satisfy is near to $\frac{1}{2}^{\lceil \log_{(1+1/\theta)} m \rceil} (1 - \frac{1}{e}) * |UTT|$, where m represents the number of clusters with the overlap among the clusters being θ. Hence, PSF does not satisfy clients, who want views greater than the above approximate value. Thus, BAF improves the revenue of the billboard operator over PSF by allocating the billboards to an increased number of clients.

The value of VA is directly proportional to the revenue of BO (since, in this paper, we convert the budget to the views). From the results in Fig. 4d, observe that BAF provides more views when compared to PSF. Hence, BAF provides more revenue to BO. In the experimental setup, we have set $maxOR$ as 0.5, which implies a minimum of 50% of the views allocated to the clients can be shown to unique user trajectories.

PSF uses the notion of overlap to divide the billboards into clusters. The billboards are divided so that the overlap between the clusters should be less than $maxOR$. From the above discussion, observe that the overlap within the cluster is maximized and the overlap between the clusters is minimized. The final output billboard set contains a set of billboards from each cluster. Billboards from different clusters satisfy the overlap rule. PSF tries to maximize the influence, i.e., unique views within the clusters. Hence, the AR of PSF is much less than BAF. Both schemes have AR less than $maxOR$, with PSF having less AR than BAF.

Nevertheless, if we reduce $maxOR$, we can guarantee that BAF outperforms PSF as the coverage patterns are generated subject to these constraints.

5.2 Effect of Varying the Number of Available Billboards

Figure 5 depicts the results for varying the number N_B of available billboards. As N_B increases, the results in Fig. 5a indicates that ET increases for both schemes. As the number of available billboards increases, the number of $UTTs$ also increases. This leads to generating more coverage patterns (in case of BAF) and more processing time (in case of PSF), thereby leading to higher values of ET. Observe that BAF incurs much lower values of ET as compared to PSF because BAF computes the coverage patterns *offline*.

As N_B increases, the results in Figs. 5b and 5c indicate that BA and CA increase for both schemes and reach a saturation point. This occurs because both schemes try to allocate billboards to the clients until all of the client requirements are satisfied. Observe that BAF utilizes almost all of the available billboards and tries to assign them to the maximum number of clients, which is not the case for PSF. Observe that in Fig. 5b, for $N_B = 10$, we utilize all the billboards

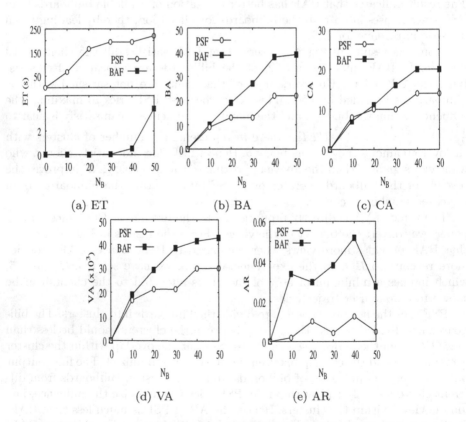

(a) ET   (b) BA   (c) CA

(d) VA   (e) AR

Fig. 5. Effect of varying the number of available billboards for GeoLife dataset

in BAF and allocate them to clients. In Fig. 5c, for $N_B = 10$, the number of clients satisfied in PSF is more than BAF. This is because BAF utilized all the billboards and allocated them to clients with a higher budget. Since most of the billboards were utilized in BAF, the value of VA in BAF is more when compared to PSF, as shown in the results in Fig. 5d.

The results in Fig. 5e indicate that both schemes satisfies $maxOR$ constraint. Nevertheless, from the discussion in Sect. 5.1, we can say that there is no trend of AR in PSF. The value of AR depends on the percentage of views repeated in the allocation since PSF minimizes the overlap between the clusters and maximizes the overlap within the cluster. If two or more billboards are allocated from the same cluster the value of AR increases. Hence, the value of AR depends on the number of clusters and the number of billboards that are taken from each cluster. In BAF, the value of AR is always less than or equal to $maxOR$ and it depends on the distribution of the billboards in the dataset.

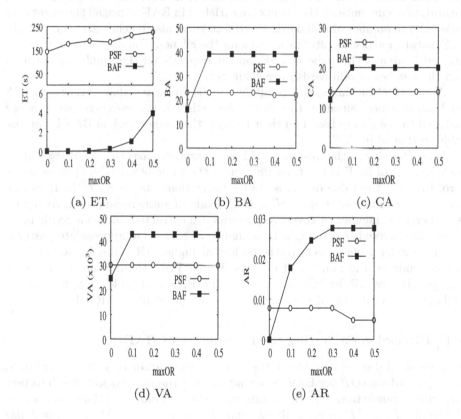

Fig. 6. Effect of varying $maxOR$ for GeoLife dataset

5.3 Effect of Varying $maxOR$

Figure 6 depicts the results for varying $maxOR$. As $maxOR$ increases, the result in Fig. 6a indicates that ET increases for both schemes. As $maxOR$ increases, the number of coverage patterns also increases, which leads to processing more patterns. Hence ET increases with $maxOR$ in BAF. ET of PSF depends on the number of clusters generated based on $maxOR$. More number of clusters leads to more ET. Since the generation of candidate patterns is offline, the value of ET for BAF is lower as compared to PSF.

When we apply stringent $maxOR$ constraint (i.e., when $maxOR < 0.1$), relatively fewer coverage patterns are generated when compared to other higher values of $maxOR$. Hence, there is lower value of BA in BAF as compared to that of PSF, which can be observed in the results of Fig. 6b. Since very few billboards are allocated, the CA and VA values are also low in BAF when $maxOR$ value is 0.0, which can be observed in Figs. 6c and 6s. From the results in Figs. 6b and 6c, saturation occurs once all the clients are satisfied in BAF. Since all the clients are satisfied, the number of billboards allotted to them also reaches to congestion. In PSF, saturation occurs after processing all the clients. The number of billboards utilized is almost the same in PSF, and it depends on the number of clusters and the number of billboards in each cluster.

As $maxOR$ increases, the result in Fig. 6d indicates that variation in VA for both schemes. Since all the clients are satisfied, i.e., coverage patterns are assigned to the clients based on their budget, the value of VA in BAF is comparable to that of in PSF.

Figure 6e shows the results of AR by varying $maxOR$. As discussed in Sect. 5.1, AR of BAF is less than PSF when the value of $maxOR$ approaches to zero. In BAF, the value of AR is always lower than that of $maxOR$. It can be noted that an increase in $maxOR$ in BAF leads to an increase in AR. At higher AR, increased number of coverage patterns are extracted and as a result more clients are covered. Also, might be a chance of allocating appropriate patterns having number of views near to the budget at higher AR value. In case of PSF, AR depends on the number of clusters. Under PSF, there is no flexibility to change AR. Overall, by varying $maxOR$, the BAF is flexible enough to assign billboards to an increased number of clients at the required AR value.

5.4 Discussion on Setting the Parameters of BAF

Now we shall discuss how to set the value of the parameters such as $minCS$, $minRF$, and $maxOR$ for BAF. Since we convert the user trajectories into user trajectory transactions, which contain only the billboard locations, we can set the value of $minRF$ as zero. Recall that the goal of our BAF is to maximize the revenue of the billboard operator (BO) by satisfying an increased number of clients. The traditional coverage pattern mining algorithm generates all the patterns with the coverage support greater than $minCS$. The value of $minCS$ can be kept as the percentage of views requirement of the client whose budget is minimum. We can start with the value of $maxOR$ as 0 and then progressively keeps increasing the value of $maxOR$ until the desired number of candidate sets of billboards are generated.

6   Conclusion

Billboards are the most widely used medium for outdoor ads. A billboard operator manages the ad slots of a set of billboards. In this paper, we have made an effort to improve the revenue of the billboard operator by efficiently allocating client ads on the billboards. We have proposed an improved billboard allocation framework (BAF) to improve the billboard operator revenue by satisfying the advertising demands of an increased number of clients. The proposed BAF is based on the user trajectory-based transactional modeling and coverage pattern mining. We have conducted experimental results on the GeoLife dataset. The results show that the proposed framework improves the revenue of the billboard operator and has better utilization of billboards over the reference approach. As part of our future work, we will explore further refinement of our proposed approach by incorporating various optimization approaches. Notably, the formulation of our problem as an optimization problem in itself poses interesting research challenges and can open new avenues for research towards further maximizing the revenue of the billboard operators. Furthermore, we plan to examine the cost-effective integration of our proposed framework into the existing billboard ad revenue business information.

References

1. Billboard Advertisement Eyeball views. http://www.runningboards.com.au/outdoor/relocatable-billboards. Accessed 1 July 2022
2. Billboard Advertisement Marketing Conversion Scheme. https://www.electro-mech.com/team-sports/advertising/billboard-advertising-cost-per-thousand-viewers/. Accessed 1 July 2022
3. Billboard Advertisement Marketing Conversion Scheme. https://www.adquick.com/billboard-cost Accessed 1 July 2022
4. U.S. Advertising Industry - Statistics & Facts. https://www.statista.com/topics/979/advertising-in-the-us/. Accessed 1 July 2022
5. Aggarwal, C.C., Yu, P.S.: A new framework for itemset generation. In: Proceedings of the ACM SIGACT-SIGMOD-SIGART Symposium on Principles of Database Systems, pp. 18–24. ACM (1998)
6. Bian, S., Guo, Q., Wang, S., Yu, J.X.: Efficient algorithms for budgeted influence maximization on massive social networks. Proce. Very Large DataBases Endowment **13**(9), 1498–1510 (2020)
7. Budhiraja, A., Ralla, A., Reddy, P.K.: Coverage pattern based framework to improve search engine advertising. Int. J. Data Sci. Analytics **8**(2), 199–211 (2018). https://doi.org/10.1007/s41060-018-0165-3
8. Domingos, P., Richardson, M.: Mining the network value of customers. In: Proceedings of the 7th ACM SIGKDD International Conference on Knowledge Discovery & Data Mining, pp. 57–66 (2001)

9. Gangumalla, L., Reddy, P.K., Mondal, A.: Multi-location visibility query processing using portion-based transactional modeling and pattern mining. Data Min. Knowl. Disc. **33**(5), 1393–1416 (2019). https://doi.org/10.1007/s10618-019-00641-3
10. Gowtham Srinivas, P., Krishna Reddy, P., Trinath, A.V., Bhargav, S., Uday Kiran, R.: Mining coverage patterns from transactional databases. J. Intell. Inf. Syst. **45**(3), 423–439 (2014). https://doi.org/10.1007/s10844-014-0318-3
11. Gray, J., Reuter, A.: Transaction Processing: Concepts and Techniques. Elsevier (1992)
12. Guo, L., Zhang, D., Cong, G., Wu, W., Tan, K.L.: Influence maximization in trajectory databases. IEEE Trans. Knowl. Data Eng. **29**(3), 627–641 (2016)
13. Huang, M., Fang, Z., Xiong, S., Zhang, T.: Interest-driven outdoor advertising display location selection using mobile phone data. IEEE Access **7**, 30878–30889 (2019)
14. Huang, M., Fang, Z., Weibel, R., Zhang, T., Huang, H.: Dynamic optimization models for displaying outdoor advertisement at the right time and place. Int. J. Geogr. Inf. Sci. **35**(6), 1179–1204 (2021)
15. Kempe, D., Kleinberg, J., Tardos, É.: Maximizing the spread of influence through a social network. In: Proceedings of the 9th ACM SIGKDD International Conference on Knowledge Discovery & Data Mining, pp. 137–146 (2003)
16. Kiran, R.U., Fournier-Viger, P., Luna, J.M., Lin, J.C.-W., Mondal, A. (eds.): Periodic Pattern Mining. Springer, Singapore (2021). https://doi.org/10.1007/978-981-16-3964-7
17. Kiran, R.U., Pallikila, P., Luna, J., Fournier-Viger, P., Toyoda, M., Reddy, P.K.: Discovering relative high utility itemsets in very large transactional databases using null-invariant measure. In: IEEE International Conference on Big Data, pp. 252–262. IEEE (2021)
18. Li, G., Chen, S., Feng, J., Tan, K.L., Li, W.S.: Efficient location-aware influence maximization. In: Proceedings of the ACM SIGMOD International Conference on Management of Data, pp. 87–98 (2014)
19. Li, Y., Fan, J., Wang, Y., Tan, K.L.: Influence maximization on social graphs: a survey. IEEE Trans. Knowl. Data Eng. **30**(10), 1852–1872 (2018)
20. Li, Y., Bao, J., Li, Y., Wu, Y., Gong, Z., Zheng, Y.: Mining the most influential k-location set from massive trajectories. IEEE Trans. Big Data **4**(4), 556–570 (2017)
21. Liu, B., Hsu, W., Ma, Y.: Mining association rules with multiple minimum supports. In: Proceedings of the 5th ACM SIGKDD International Conference on Knowledge Discovery & Data Mining, pp. 337–341 (1999)
22. Liu, D., et al.: SmartAdP: visual analytics of large-scale taxi trajectories for selecting billboard locations. IEEE Trans. Visual Comput. Graph. **23**(1), 1–10 (2016)
23. Lou, K., Yang, Y., Wang, E., Liu, Z., Baker, T., Bashir, A.K.: Reinforcement learning based advertising strategy using crowdsensing vehicular data. IEEE Trans. Intell. Transp. Syst. **22**(7), 1–13 (2020)
24. Ralla, A., Siddiqie, S., Reddy, P.K., Mondal, A.: Coverage pattern mining based on MapReduce. In: Proceedings of the ACM International Conference on Data Science and Management of Data, pp. 209–213 (2020)
25. Rathan, P.R., Reddy, P.K., Mondal, A.: Improving billboard advertising revenue using transactional modeling and pattern mining. In: Strauss, C., Kotsis, G., Tjoa, A.M., Khalil, I. (eds.) DEXA 2021. LNCS, vol. 12923, pp. 112–118. Springer, Cham (2021). https://doi.org/10.1007/978-3-030-86472-9_10
26. Richardson, M., Domingos, P.: Mining knowledge-sharing sites for viral marketing. In: Proceedings of the 8th ACM SIGKDD International Conference on Knowledge Discovery & Data Mining, pp. 61–70 (2002)

27. Srinivas, P.G., Reddy, P.K., Bhargav, S., Kiran, R.U., Kumar, D.S.: Discovering coverage patterns for banner advertisement placement. In: Tan, P.-N., Chawla, S., Ho, C.K., Bailey, J. (eds.) PAKDD 2012. LNCS (LNAI), vol. 7302, pp. 133–144. Springer, Heidelberg (2012). https://doi.org/10.1007/978-3-642-30220-6_12

28. Wang, L., Yu, Z., Yang, D., Ma, H., Sheng, H.: Efficiently targeted billboard advertising using crowdsensing vehicle trajectory data. IEEE Trans. Industr. Inf. **16**(2), 1058–1066 (2020)

29. Wu, T.Y., Lin, J.C.W., Yun, U., Chen, C.H., Srivastava, G., Lv, X.: An efficient algorithm for fuzzy frequent itemset mining. J. Intell. Fuzzy Syst. **38**(5), 5787–5797 (2020)

30. Wu, Y., Luo, L., Li, Y., Guo, L., Fournier-Viger, P., Zhu, X., Wu, X.: Ntp-miner: nonoverlapping three-way sequential pattern mining. ACM Trans. Knowl. Discov. Data **16**(3), 1–21 (2021)

31. Zhang, P., Bao, Z., Li, Y., Li, G., Zhang, Y., Peng, Z.: Trajectory-driven influential billboard placement. In: Proceedings of the 24th ACM SIGKDD International Conference on Knowledge Discovery & Data Mining, pp. 2748–2757 (2018)

32. Zhang, Y., Li, Y., Bao, Z., Mo, S., Zhang, P.: Optimizing impression counts for outdoor advertising. In: Proceedings of the 25th ACM SIGKDD International Conference on Knowledge Discovery & Data Mining, pp. 1205–1215 (2019)

33. Zheng, Y., Xie, X., Ma, W.Y.: GeoLife: a collaborative social networking service among user, location and trajectory. IEEE Database Eng. Bull. **33**(2), 32–39 (2010)

Author Index

Printed in the United States
by Baker & Taylor Publisher Services

Printed in the United States
by Baker & Taylor Publisher Services